THE
FOOD
MATTERS
COOKBOOK

THE
FOOD
MATTERS
COOKBOOK

A Simple Gluten-Free Guide
to Transforming Your Health
One Meal at a Time

JAMES COLQUHOUN & LAURENTINE TEN BOSCH

HAY HOUSE, INC.
Carlsbad, California • New York City
London • Sydney • New Delhi

Copyright © 2022 by Food Matters Holdings Pty Ltd

Published in the United States by: Hay House, Inc.:
www.hayhouse.com® • *Published in Australia by:*
Hay House Australia Pty. Ltd.: www.hayhouse.com.au •
Published in the United Kingdom by: Hay House UK, Ltd.:
www.hayhouse.co.uk • *Published in India by:*
Hay House Publishers India: www.hayhouse.co.in

INDEXER: Joan Shapiro
COVER DESIGN: Stephanie Kennerson
INTERIOR DESIGN: Shubhani Sarkar, sarkardesignstudio.com
INTERIOR PHOTOGRAPHY: Chloe Hutchison

Cataloging-in-Publication Data is on file at the Library of
Congress

Hardcover ISBN: 978-1-4019-6753-6
E-book ISBN: 978-1-4019-6754-3

10 9 8 7 6 5 4 3 2 1

1st edition, April 2022

Printed in the United States of America

SFI label applies to the text stock

You know how it is. You pick up a book, open to the dedication, and find that, once again, the authors have dedicated a book to someone else and not to you.

Not this time.

This book is for you. Every handcrafted recipe and every detailed piece of health research condensed into a bite-size usable form is all for you.

This information helped to save my father's life, and it's my wish that it might help to save yours, or that of someone you love. At the very least I hope it makes your tastebuds sing, improves your mood, and boosts your energy!

This one's for you.

With love and respect,

JAMES & LAURENTINE

CONTENTS

YOU ARE WHAT YOU EAT

CAN CHANGING WHAT YOU EAT REALLY CHANGE YOUR LIFE?

At Food Matters, we firmly believe that you are what you eat. We know this because we've seen it firsthand.

In 2003, my father, Roy, was diagnosed with chronic fatigue syndrome—one of a growing list of mystery illnesses that have no specific known cause or treatment, according to the medical profession. At the time, we didn't realize how much this was going to impact our lives. We thought we could outsource his treatment to our family doctor and move on. How wrong we were . . .

For the next five years, most of his days were spent in bed, and his nights were often filled with sweaty panic attacks, the anticipated side effects of his medications. He had gained more than 50 pounds, was increasingly lethargic, and suffered from depression.

Not one medical professional suggested he change his diet or eating habits, nor did they recommend different ways to handle stress. Not surprisingly, his health began to deteriorate further.

We knew we had to intervene. But every attempt to help was met with keen resistance.

We got ahold of every book we could find and started researching. We soon learned that healthy food and the power of nutrition could be used to heal. We also discovered that our health care, food, and agricultural industries were not particularly concerned with our health. They were primarily interested in profits. We couldn't believe what we were uncovering. Our new discoveries inspired us to formalize our knowledge through studying nutrition online to gain the tools to help heal my father.

At first, there were more questions than answers. Why didn't my father's doctor know about the power of nutrition and natural therapies to heal? And why were we not taught this in school? But slowly we started to see the bigger picture.

Studying nutrition led to us traveling the world interviewing many of the experts we had been studying to create the *Food Matters* film. While we struggled with interventions and couldn't motivate my father to read a 300-page book on natural healing, we figured we could probably convince him to watch a film.

BEFORE

AFTER

We invested our life's savings into the making of *Food Matters*, traveling from Holland (Laurentine's home country) and England to the East and West Coasts of the United States, and then Australia (James's home country), interviewing doctors, nutritionists, scientists, and wellness experts on how to heal the body naturally.

We brought all the footage home to my father and proclaimed that we weren't leaving the house until he got well. Before long, he was hooked. What stood out, he told us later, was the story of how one of the medications he was on had been known to cause suicidal thoughts. This was his worst fear and something he had recently been experiencing.

Not only was the current approach not helping him, it was making him worse. Almost immediately, through access to this new information, he had a paradigm shift. He went from believing in a fully drug-

based approach to healing, to believing in his body's innate capacity to heal itself.

As Andrew Saul, Ph.D., from *Food Matters* says, "*We need education, not medication.*"

Now that he was on board, we began a pantry audit to contraband all the fake and processed food that wasn't real. This included many so-called "health foods" and "diet products," all the processed foods and refined vegetable oils, and all the factory-farmed meat and dairy. We then guided him through a clean-eating program by adding more and more healthy foods to his diet.

Within weeks, his energy started to return. He was out of bed, moving freely and energetically around the house. He regained confidence in the kitchen again, creating healthy and delicious meals made from scratch using real, whole-food ingredients. After five years of daily medication, within one month he was off all of his meds and experienced zero side effects or withdrawal symptoms. Within three months, he had lost 50 pounds, was no longer anxious or depressed, was sleeping through the night, and woke up each morning refreshed and ready for the day. He even started running and exercising again, something he hadn't done in years. He was a completely transformed version of himself.

It was one of the most amazing transformations I have ever witnessed. And as a positive side effect, we had my father back, and our family became closer than it had ever been before.

Laurentine and I knew that this information was powerful and that we had to share this knowledge and the documentary with as many people as possible. Since the film's release in 2008, *Food Matters* has been seen by millions of people online, in theaters, on television, on airlines, and even in hospitals and community centers around the world, from Connecticut to Cambodia, in nine different languages.

After *Food Matters* was released, we went on to produce three more documentaries, including *Hungry for Change* and *Transcendence* seasons 1 and 2, most of which have been featured on Netflix, Gaia, and iTunes, and are available to stream on FoodMatters.com.

To this day, we feel grateful to have helped my father turn his life around and inspire a community of millions around the world to do the same.

This book is a collection of the principles, philosophies, and research we gained from my father's transformation and continued to discover over the years from the incredible teachers with whom we have worked.

Over the following pages, we'll be going on a journey together. While you could simply pick up this cookbook and jump straight to the recipes, we want to help you not only improve your kitchen skills but also discover what actually makes these recipes healthy and how you can create lasting health and well-being outside of the health-care industry. In Part I you'll learn more about the Food Matters story and what inspired this movement and be introduced to our team and vision for this book. Then in Part II we share with you our foundational nutrition principles, how your body benefits from eating more whole foods, daily rituals and habits that will set you up for success, and how to help heal your gut and digestion naturally. We will also explore some of the non-food elements of the Food Matters philosophy, including the importance of slowing down and returning to nature and how this can benefit our overall well-being.

Part III is all about preparing your kitchen to set you up for daily success, including healthy swaps for common unhealthy foods, minimizing food waste, and stocking your pantry for all seasons, plus essential equipment to make your healthy eating journey easier. In Part IV we dive headfirst into the recipes from juices and smoothies to healthy snacks, mains, and the all-important desserts! And finally, in Part V, we've created a seven-day meal plan to help you make all the information in the book as practical as possible.

We believe that your body is worthy of good care and that nobody is more suitably qualified to care for it than yourself. We're just here to help!

In good health,

JAMES COLQUHOUN &
LAURENTINE TEN BOSCH

"PEOPLE ARE FED BY THE FOOD INDUSTRY, WHICH PAYS NO ATTENTION TO HEALTH, AND ARE HEALED BY THE HEALTH INDUSTRY, WHICH PAYS NO ATTENTION TO FOOD."

— WENDELL BERRY

YOUR NUTRITION COACHES

"If I have seen further,
it is by standing on the shoulders of giants."

— ISAAC NEWTON

THE FOOD MATTERS TEACHERS

This book, the Food Matters films, and all recipes have been inspired by the groundbreaking research and dedication of the incredible teachers we have had the opportunity to work with over the past 15 years. Special thanks go out to Mark Hyman, M.D.; John Robbins; Anthony "The Medical Medium" William; David Wolfe; Kris Carr; Charlotte Gerson; Libby Weaver, Ph.D.; Dave Asprey; Jason Vale; Bruce Lipton, Ph.D.; Joe Dispenza, D.C.; Rich Roll; Gabrielle Bernstein; Jon Gabriel; Chris Wark; Joe Cross; Josh Axe, D.N.M., D.C., C.N.S.; Vani "Food Babe" Hari; Daniel Vitalis; Ocean Robbins; and many more. This book brings together their great work into a single practical daily guide to nourishing yourself, with delicious recipes that help you navigate the confusion around what to eat and what to avoid.

JAMES COLQUHOUN

Hi, I'm James Colquhoun—filmmaker, gardener, surfer, cook, and conscious entrepreneur. In 2008 Laurentine and I co-founded FoodMatters.com, a global wellness hub that has inspired millions around the world to upgrade their habits, lose weight naturally, and transform their health. My path to wellness certainly wasn't a conventional one. After watching my father suffer from chronic illnesses, I was inspired to study nutrition online and went on to co-produce four internationally acclaimed documentary films: *Food Matters* (2008), *Hungry for Change* (2012), and *Transcendence*, season 1 (2018) and season 2 (2020). In that time I have co-authored multiple books and helped to build an online community of over 4 million followers. In 2014 we launched Food Matters TV (FMTV), known as the "Netflix for wellness," which grew to over 1,800 titles and over 900 hours of content before merging with Gaia to create the world's largest transformational streaming network, for which I am an active board member. My mission is to continue to provide life-changing education to help people take charge of their life and health. I love spending my time reading inspirational and spiritual books; deepening my yoga and meditation practices; and helping give back through our Food Matters Foundation with community projects in Fiji, Vanuatu, Bali, and beyond. I believe that if you have your health, you can have 1,000 goals, but without your health you have only one goal—getting healthy. May this book help you to eat well, live well, and serve others.

LAURENTINE TEN BOSCH

Hi, I'm Laurentine ten Bosch—filmmaker, nutritionist, author, conscious parent, and builder of nature schools! I am originally from Holland, but I've grown up in many different countries and have always had a passion for international food and culture. After studying nutrition, I became fascinated with our bodies' innate capacity for self-healing. From our journey of producing the Food Matters films to co-creating the online wellness hub FoodMatters.com with a global online community, I love remaining connected to the real stories of people changing their lives day by day and the incredible results that can come from taking simple steps to improving your health. Recently I returned to my roots in Vanuatu, a small Pacific island where I spent a large portion of my childhood, and it is where I have been transitioning into following my passion more deeply into education. Here I have been founding a nature school

through the Food Matters Foundation, helping to create a strong, thriving, and healthy community for generations to come. While living on a remote island in the Pacific, I eat an abundance of delicious seasonal foods, shop local markets, cook traditional meals, and enjoy foods in their most natural, wholesome state. I hope the recipes in this book help inspire you to embrace this natural and simplistic style of living and create healthy habits for you and your loved ones.

RACHEL MORROW

Hi, I'm Rachel Morrow—recipe developer and content creator at Food Matters. My love for cooking and creating recipes came at a young age from experimenting in the kitchen, not following recipes, and seeing what I could create, albeit with some disasters and occasional smoke alarms. But I learned a lot, and fast. My love and interest for food and health led me to earn a bachelor of nutrition at the University of the Sunshine Coast. All the while, I had this feeling deep down inside that I wasn't going to be someone who could follow the mainstream health guidelines, and I started to seek a more holistic path. On that journey, I came across James and Laurentine and the work they were doing around a film they had just released. That's when I joined what we now call the "Food Matters Family," and I've become one of the longest-serving team members. Early on, when the company was just starting, I took a role in customer support, and I was introduced to a global community and experienced firsthand the challenges people were facing with their health. Ten years on, I have transitioned to growing and managing our social media community of over 4 million followers and creating content and delicious recipes for our amazing followers. One of the recurring requests from our community is for quick and healthy recipes that the whole family will love that will also not break the piggy bank. I also love helping people find creative ways to keep meals healthy and exciting that are also gluten-free, dairy-free, and easy to digest. My wish is to remove the perception of healthy cooking being too difficult, with impossible-to-find, expensive wellness ingredients. I want to share my love for fresh, vibrant, and nourishing ingredients with you and help you fall in love with cooking for your family, your health, and, most importantly, your taste buds!

FOOD MATTERS TEAM

"Never doubt that a small group of thoughtful, committed citizens can change the world; indeed, it's the only thing that ever has."

— MARGARET MEAD

The creation of this recipe book would not have been possible without the team at Food Matters. And if there's one thing the team loves, it's delicious food, so you can rest assured that nothing but the best recipes and lifestyle advice have gone into this book from beginning to end. Our team is dedicated to helping support you on your journey to better health and ultimately for you to become a radiant beacon of health in your own family and community.

Special thanks to Ivette Rieksts for helping to create the recipes and design throughout the recipe book; Chloe Hutchison for photography and an amazing vision; Peita Ward for all the behind-the-scenes work to bring the project together; Tessa Patrick for always weaving her magic with the words behind these pages; and the rest of the team for all the love and dedication that went into this project.

At Food Matters, we're so much more than just delicious, nourishing foods. Our story has evolved, but our mission remains the same: to share this life-changing message with more people. Food Matters has focused this vision around three core values. The journey begins with transformation, where our guided programs offer people the opportunity to take back their health.

We know that education is the most incredible tool for change, so we built upon the knowledge from our films, books, podcasts, and interviews to build the Food Matters Institute, which offers our nutrition certification program to share the importance of the power of nutrition. Lastly, we have you, our Food Matters community. We've fostered a thriving global community, who come together to share their transformational journeys and encourage us to keep sharing this message.

Eating for health includes knowing where your food comes from, how your food is prepared, and how the ingredients you choose can impact your energy, digestion, and mood. In this section you'll gain an understanding of the Food Matters philosophy and simple ways to apply these principles to your own life.

EATING FOR HEALTH

10 FOOD MATTERS NUTRITION PRINCIPLES

1. EAT AS NATURE INTENDED

Nature didn't create you to eat frozen ready-made meals with artificial preservatives and chemicals. Our ancestors have always lived in harmony with nature, and we are designed to eat as nature intended. Pure, natural, and organic foods direct from the farm to your table. Many of the longest-living, healthiest, and happiest people on planet Earth alive today eat plenty of vegetables and fruits, herbs, seaweeds, superfoods, mushrooms, sprouted nuts and seeds, activated grains and pseudograins, live-cultured foods and fermented vegetables, and occasionally small amounts of free-range eggs, wild fish, and game.

2. CHOOSE ORGANIC WHEN POSSIBLE

Organic fruits and vegetables contain more vitamins and minerals than their non-organic counterparts, particularly if they are picked ripe and locally grown.

Moreover, they are safer to eat as they are grown without the use of chemical fertilizers, pesticides, and genetically modified organisms, all of which may have harmful long-term effects on our reproductive health and hormones, as well as overloading the liver with harmful toxins. Throughout this book we recommend choosing organic ingredients wherever possible. If animal products are in your diet, we encourage you to choose sustainably farmed, organic meat and products. This includes sustainably sourced fish, pastured-raised and free-range eggs, and grass-fed, ethically raised animal products.

3. LIMIT YOUR INTAKE OF GLUTEN-CONTAINING GRAINS

Gluten is a protein found in many grains, namely wheat, rye, barley, triticale, and contaminated oats. Gluten may irritate and damage the intestinal lining, causing inflammation, and may result in an autoimmune response that contributes to increased intestinal permeability, commonly referred to as "leaky gut." Because of the domestication and genetic modification of modern wheat and its increased consumption in the Western diet, celiac disease, gluten intolerance, and gluten sensitivity are becoming more prevalent. In this book, we've compiled our recipes with gluten-free grains so everyone can enjoy them, especially those who can't live without pancakes, bread, and cookies!

4. STEER CLEAR OF PROCESSED SUGAR

Too much sugar or other refined "simple" carbohydrates can lead to blood sugar highs and lows, causing mood swings and food cravings and possibly contributing to obesity and chronic disease. Consuming large amounts of refined sugar is associated with a greater risk of fatty liver disease, insulin resistance, heart disease, and type 2 diabetes. The solution: opt for foods that naturally have a lower glycemic load or a low glycemic index (GI), and avoid sweetened packaged foods, particularly those sweetened with high-fructose corn syrup (HFCS), corn and glucose syrups, and artificial sweeteners. In this book, we use natural sweeteners such as dates, honey, and pure maple syrup.

5. EAT GOOD FATS

People who are trying to lose weight often try to keep their fat intake to a minimum. The reason behind this is that fat contains more calories per gram than carbohydrates and proteins. However, good fats are essential for the absorption of most nutrients, as well as for satiating hunger and for the production of hormones—so, it's actually important not to avoid them. Here at Food Matters, we believe in counting nutrients, not calories! We'll help you to make a healthy relationship with the fats found in hemp seeds, chia seeds, flaxseeds, Brazil nuts, almonds, walnuts, coconut oil, extra virgin cold-pressed olive oil, macadamia nuts, and avocados, and, additionally for non-vegans, select high-quality wild-caught

fish, ghee, butter, and grass-fed meats. Make sure you steer clear of the oxidized, free-radical-creating trans fats found in margarine spreads, cookies, chips, factory-farmed meat, and refined, processed vegetable oils such as safflower, sunflower, and canola oil.

6. BE SMART IN THE KITCHEN

Prepare your meals with care. Ditch the microwave. Eat more raw, living foods. Don't burn your foods but rather steam or sauté them in heat-stable fats over low to medium heat. Get an old-fashioned cast-iron pot and learn how to slow cook. Ditch the Teflon and nonstick pans. Ferment your veggies. Compost your scraps. Ditch the plastic wrap. And stock your pantry

with health-promoting foods to help support your transformation. Soak and activate your nuts. We'll expand more on preparing your kitchen in Part III.

7. DUST OFF YOUR JUICER AND BLENDER

A juicer or blender can be your best friend in the kitchen, making it easier for you to up the intake of vegetables and fruits in your diet. This will help you to naturally crowd out the foods that can have a harmful effect on your body. Let's say you come home from work and you are feeling hungry and lethargic. You might normally reach for a bag of chips or cookies, but with your juicer, blender, and selection of quick, delicious, and easy recipes handy, you'll be nourishing your body with a cold-pressed juice or smoothie loaded with vitamins, minerals, and enzymes. This is our kind of instant meal!

8. SHOP FOR ETHICAL AND SUSTAINABLE SOURCES

When buying fresh produce, fish, eggs, and other animal products, it's important to choose sustainable sources and to know where your food comes from. Toxins and chemicals tend to accumulate mostly within fat cells; therefore, sourcing organically grown nuts, seeds, oils, and animal products is best. With organic and free-range animal products, it is reassuring to know that there are no antibiotics, growth hormones, or GMO products used in the production process. If in doubt, ask your local food supplier or farmer some simple questions; if they have nothing to hide, they will always be happy to help.

9. AVOID FOOD ADDITIVES

Read your food labels! Chemical food additives can wreak havoc on our hormones. In general, avoid E numbers (these are codes for common food additives) but be particularly careful with the flavor enhancer MSG, which tricks our brains into thinking we need to overeat. MSG is disguised under the following names: E621, monosodium glutamate, glutamic acid, hydrolyzed vegetable

oil, yeast extract, and monocalcium glutamate. It is often found in ready-made soups, chips, sauces, and cookies. As a general rule: if you can't pronounce it or it's listed in numbers or code, don't eat it!

10. EAT IN A RELAXED STATE

Our stomach and digestive systems are very sensitive. Rushing your meal and eating on the run will put your body in a state of fight or flight, which in turn will compromise or even halt your digestive processes and the uptake of nutrients. What we don't digest can turn into bacterial fermentation or bloating, or, worst of all, it can be stored for later (aka fat and cellulite in the places we want it least). Make sure you are seated and take the time to enjoy your meal in a relaxed state with a peaceful intention. We like to say a quick blessing before we eat a meal, to give thanks, and to take a few deep breaths to calm our bodies.

THE CASE FOR EATING MORE WHOLE FOODS

Whether you want to reduce the level of processed foods, meat, or sugar in your diet, there are many benefits for having more whole plant-based foods for your health, the environment, animals, and society overall.

When we talk about plant-based diets, we mean meals based primarily on whole vegetables, legumes, fruits, nuts, seeds, and grains, while at the same time limiting processed foods, factory-farmed meat, dairy, and animal products, and even some plants and grains that can irritate the gut or impair nutrient absorption.

While it seems to be constantly growing in popularity online and in food stores, adopting a plant-based diet is more than just a trendy way to eat; it's actually backed by scientific research.

A report compiled by a group of 30 nutrition scientists from around the world, published in the British medical journal *The Lancet*, recommends a largely plant-based diet, with small, occasional allowances for meat, dairy, and sugar.[1] This would allow healthy diets that enable the growing population of the Earth to be fed while managing factors such as greenhouse gas emissions, water use, crop use, land use, and more.

And if you're looking for more inspiration, here are nine reasons to introduce more easily digestible, whole plant-based foods into your diet.

1. CUT YOUR CARBON FOOTPRINT BY 50 PERCENT OR MORE

The amount of resources it takes to produce one pound of beef is astonishing and contributes significantly to global warming, according to a major report by the Intergovernmental Panel on Climate Change, a body of the United Nations.

Fifteen pounds of grain are required to produce one pound of beef, and the amount of beef the average American consumes in a year creates greenhouse gases equivalent to driving a car 1,800 miles.[2] Switching to a plant-based diet with just two-thirds of your weekly meals completely vegan could see your personal carbon footprint reduced by almost 60 percent.

2. SAVE GALLONS OF WATER

Huge amounts of water are needed to raise animals for food, and just a fraction of that amount of water is required to grow plants and grains. In fact, nearly half of all the water used in the United States goes to livestock.

A typical meat-eater diet racks up 4,000 gallons of water per day in associated preparation and production, but only 300 gallons of water are used to produce a day's food for a typical vegan.[3]

You could save more water by not eating a pound of meat than you would by not showering for six months.

Additionally, if you switched your daily tea to have oat milk instead of cow milk, and you had two cups per day, over a year you would save over 22,000 gallons of water. That's the equivalent of 108 showers of 8 minutes duration.

3. LOSE WEIGHT

Plants are low in calories, high in fiber, rich in health-promoting phytochemicals, and help you feel fuller on less food, keeping your bowels regular and allowing your body to absorb more nutrients with less effort.

Studies[4] have shown that following a plant-based diet is effective in treating obesity, and those on a plant-based or vegan diet have the lowest average BMI (body mass index).

4. REDUCE INFLAMMATION

If you regularly consume conventional meat, dairy, and processed foods, it's highly likely you've got a lot of inflammation in your body because of the unhealthy fats and endotoxins in these products. Inflammation is the body's response and a warning sign to you that there is something harmful that the body has encountered. Inflammation is helpful and necessary in the short term, but long-lasting or chronic inflammation can be linked to a wide range of chronic diseases.

Studies[5] have shown that switching to a plant-based diet provides you with natural anti-inflammatory benefits to reduce your current inflammation. Plus, there are far fewer inflammatory catalysts present in fruit, vegetables, nuts, and seeds. Some of our favorites are green leafy vegetables, hemp seeds, walnuts, and avocado—which all come together to make the beautiful Skin Beauty Salad (page 238).

5. HAVE MORE ENERGY

Well-prepared plant-based meals are generally more easily digested and their nutrients quickly absorbed into the body, and as a result you can experience a fast injection of energy that lasts. Having more energy can improve your mental and physical health by enabling you to participate in more activities of your choosing. Instead of a block of refined-sugar chocolate, reach for one of our Energy Bliss Ball recipes (page 329) for your afternoon pick-me-up.

6. DEVELOP RADIANT SKIN

Eating a clean diet rich in vegetables, fruits, nuts, and seeds not only has a great detoxifying effect to clear the skin but also provides incredible nutrients to see you heal and glow from the inside out. The nutrient boost of vitamins C, E, and B-complex, and zinc, copper, and selenium can help make hair shiny and skin clear and radiant, smooth wrinkles, and protect your skin from the sun.[6]

Avocado, a fruit rich in healthy fats and vitamins, does wonders for both our hair and skin. Plus, it tastes just as good in smoothies and rice paper rolls as it does on our gluten-free bread! Find it in our Food Matters Signature Green Smoothie (page 76) or with our Rice Paper Rolls with Tamari Dipping Sauce (page 140).

7. REDUCE CHOLESTEROL LEVELS AND RISK OF CARDIOVASCULAR DISEASE

Studies[7] show that a plant-based diet is a remarkably effective intervention in lowering plasma cholesterol concentrations. Results from case studies have shown outcomes as dramatic as a 35 percent reduction in blood cholesterol levels. This is predominantly because of the low amounts of unhealthy fats in plants compared with conventionally grown animal products.

With a growing global vegan population, there are now supermarket shelves of substitutes, but some of our favorite meat substitutes are made at home with lentils and mushrooms, used in our Mushroom & Lentil Bolognese (page 171).

8. REDUCE THE RISK OF DISEASE

Whole-food plant-based diets are a rich source of vitamins, minerals, fiber, protein, and healthy fats that promote good health.

Large prospective trials[8] have found that populations that follow plant-based diets, particularly vegetarian and vegan diets, are at lower risk of death from ischemic heart disease.

A study[9] on the impact of diet and type 2 diabetes found that plant-based diets, especially when rich in high-quality plant foods, are associated with a substantially lower risk of developing type 2 diabetes.

Additionally, the American Cancer Society Guidelines on Nutrition and Physical Activity for cancer prevention[10] promotes a diet that emphasizes plant-based food and avoidance of red and processed meat.

9. SAVE MONEY

Buying meat as part of your weekly shopping can be quite expensive, and so too are medical bills that can follow a processed foods and conventional meat-heavy diet. There is often a perception that healthy, plant-based food is expensive. But try using a handful of vegetables and some fragrant herbs and spices as your catalyst to get creative in the kitchen. If you make your meals at home from good individual ingredients rather than prepackaged meat alternatives, you may end up saving more money than you expect, and you might even want to treat yourself to an extra smoothie or gluten-free treat like our Nut Butter Fudge (page 303) over the weekend.

Whether you choose to ditch animal products for the environment, your health, or for the well-being of animals, there are plenty of great reasons that show you can make a positive change by choosing to add more whole-food plant-based recipes into your weekly routine.

OUR SIX FAVORITE
DOCTORS ARE:
SUNSHINE. REST.
REAL FOOD. WATER.
AIR. MOVEMENT.

CREATING HEALTHY HABITS AND MORNING RITUALS

Creating healthy habits and morning rituals is a great place to start when transforming your health and wellness. Implementing these new habits into your morning can help take you from struggling to get out of bed and reaching for the coffeepot, to waking up before your alarm with more energy. When practiced daily, the smallest habits can help increase your energy levels, support immune function, improve mental focus and clarity, decrease that sluggish and bloated feeling, and help start your day off in the best possible way.

LEMON WATER

Upon rising, rehydrate your body and cells with a large glass of filtered room-temperature water with freshly squeezed lemon or lime to cleanse your body and stimulate digestion. Out of citrus? A big glass of filtered water is still a great way to hydrate your body and flush out toxins. If you want to take this morning ritual to another level, try adding some cayenne pepper, apple cider vinegar, or freshly juiced ginger or turmeric.

MOVE YOUR BODY

Taking 10 minutes to move your body in the morning can help to get your energy flowing and set you up for a positive day. Try a short yoga class, a walk on the beach or around your neighborhood, a strengthening Pilates class, or even a fast high-intensity workout. Like your diet, what works for you will be different from what works for others, and this may change over time.

JUST BREATHE

Take at least one minute to consciously breathe before you start your day. The simpler, the better. Focus on deep diaphragmatic breathing (when your belly moves up and down) to activate your parasympathetic nervous system, which is responsible for helping you to "rest, digest, and repair." You can do this most simply by breathing through your nose and bringing the following qualities to your breath: deep, rhythmic, smooth, seamless, and silent.

MEDITATE

Once you've finished moving your body and centering your focus on your breath it's time to still your mind, lay in Savasana (on your back) or take a cross-legged position with your spine erect, and take a few moments of meditation to calm your mind and create your ideal day. If you struggle to meditate and calm your mind, try the simple practice of focusing your attention on the mantra so hum. Imagine silently chanting so on the in breath and

hum on the out breath. This will keep your mind in one place and allow you to relax more fully into the practice.

COLD EXPOSURE

Stimulate your body's immunity and kick-start your energy without the need for coffee with at least 10 seconds of a cold-water shower or a plunge into a nearby ocean, river, or lake. Don't worry, you can start with a hot shower—just make sure to finish cold.

NOURISH YOUR BODY

When you enter your kitchen after your morning rituals, it's time to make a nourishing breakfast to set your cells up for success during the day. The key is to not overcomplicate it. If you feel like having a green juice or some low-sugar fruit, now's the time while you still have an empty stomach. After that, you're onto a nourishing breakfast with a combination of high-quality fats, fiber, and protein.

PRACTICE GRATITUDE

Whether you're just taking a moment to think about something you're grateful for or writing in a journal, practicing gratitude first thing in the morning can have a profound impact on your day. This action can lead to an increase in serotonin—the happiness hormone—which leads to positive relationships with those around you, and with yourself, which in turn can result in a decrease in thoughts of depression.

11 SIGNS OF AN UNHEALTHY GUT

Here are a few telltale signs that your gut is in need of some tender loving care from you. On the surface, these may not seem like they need urgent attention, but if left uncared for over a period of time, they can lead to larger complications. Your gut is an area to always pay attention to and take active steps to providing extra nutrients and care.

- BLOATING
- FOOD SENSITIVITIES
- DIGESTIVE PROBLEMS: IBS & LEAKY GUT
- THYROID CONDITIONS
- SKIN ISSUES: ROSACEA & ACNE
- HEADACHES
- JOINT PAIN
- WEIGHT CHANGE: GAIN OR IRREGULAR LOSS
- FOOD CRAVINGS: SUGAR & CARBS
- MOOD ISSUES
- FATIGUE

GOOD HEALTH BEGINS IN THE GUT

Your gut is a delicate ecosystem, with more flora (healthy bacteria) contained within it than all the other cells in the body combined. That's a lot of flora!

When this ecosystem is healthy and flourishing, your digestive tract has the proper balance of stomach acids and bacteria. This perfect balance allows your body to break down food for nourishment and cell repair.

Without the ability to absorb nutrition from your food and eliminate waste, you may experience all kinds of health issues that, on the surface, don't seem to be related to your digestion, but quite likely are.

Whether you suffer from headaches, mood issues, weight gain, menstrual cramps, fatigue, back pain, frequent colds, estrogen dominance, and many more, these are all issues that could be caused by having a seriously unhappy gut.

Simply put, if your gut is suffering, everything else suffers too.

HOW YOUR GUT WORKS

Did you know that your gut is technically outside your body?

Sure, this sounds extremely strange, but technically we have one long tube running through our body. The term for this tube is the "alimentary canal," and it is made up of the mouth, esophagus, stomach, intestines, and anus.

This tube is pinched closed by your mouth, anus, and certain sphincters along the digestive tract. However, technically this canal is not completely and permanently sealed shut from the outside world. So, from a physiological perspective, we say it is outside of your body. Unbelievable, right?

The gut is "outside" of our body for a very important immunological reason: our environment is naturally filled with billions of bacteria. This is not to scare you, as bacteria play a very important role in sustaining life on Earth. However, our body is not equipped to let any ol' bug from the outside world into our bloodstream.

Therefore, our gut contains a very sophisticated immune system to make sure that the bugs that we swallow and eat are not given free rein into our bloodstream.

WHAT AFFECTS OUR GUT HEALTH?

When it comes to gut health, it's not just food that can cause our flora to become imbalanced. Many factors in our modern environment negatively impact our gut health.

The residual chemicals from pesticides, herbicides, and other agricultural chemicals wind up in our gut when we eat non-organic food and hurt our friendly tummy bugs too. Agricultural runoff makes its way into our waterways, so unfiltered water can also be contaminated with compounds that reduce our gut flora.

WHAT IS LEAKY GUT?

Leaky gut syndrome, also referred to as intestinal permeability or hyperpermeability, is a condition where the "gatekeepers" within your gut are not properly working to control what passes through to the small intestine. This means that harmful elements such as proteins (including gluten), undigested particles, and bad bacteria are able to leak into your bloodstream.

What may not seem harmful in the short term can have profound effects on your health in the long term. These particles can wreak havoc by causing inflammation and immune reactions over time.

Your small intestine may be little, but it is a mighty organ with incredibly important functions. It helps to absorb the majority of nutrients, such as vitamins and minerals, from your food. With a healthy gut, the small intestine contains small junctions that allow for vital nutrients to be deposited around the body by the bloodstream. If it's in working order, it will only allow certain elements to enter the bloodstream and will block toxic elements from entering. Think of it as the bodyguard to your bloodstream, only letting the VIPs into the bloodstream club.

However, with a leaky gut, these small openings within your small intestine are widened. This then allows for all sorts of undigested food particles and toxins to take a ride through your bloodstream and can lead to inflammation and immune reactions.

Some of the initial signs that you may have a leaky gut include food allergies, digestive issues (IBS, bloating, diarrhea), and skin issues such as eczema and acne.

8 DAILY HABITS FOR A HEALTHY GUT

It's the small things that add up to make big changes to how we feel! Try out these 8 simple steps to build a happier, healthier belly!

1. REMOVE IRRITANTS

Looking after your gut health doesn't just mean focusing on what healthy foods you should be eating; we need to first focus on removing common gut irritants. These are the things that are causing inflammation in our digestive systems and damaging the lining of our guts, leading to nutrients not being absorbed and our guts not functioning properly. One of the biggest irritants we need to eliminate is genetically modified organisms (GMOs). Unfortunately, through the genetically modified farming that has swept the globe, the human population has been exposed to more pesticides and chemicals than ever before. From affecting the microbiome in our soils to the microbiome in our guts, this is only a small caution to what GMOs can really do to our health. Choosing locally grown organic produce is the best way to avoid this, along with limiting packaged genetically modified foods. Other common irritants include refined sugars, gluten, alcohol, and antibiotics.[11]

2. SOOTHE YOUR GUT LINING

Relieving inflammation is the next step to take in soothing the gut lining. Increasing your omega-3 intake through foods such as chia seeds, flaxseeds, and wild-caught fish will help to reduce inflammation in the lining of your gut.[12] Restorative broths are rich in vitamins and minerals and are a direct source of collagen, chondroitin, and glucosamine, which can help to "heal and seal" the lining of the digestive tract. (Try our Restorative Broth recipe, page 272.) Additionally, aloe vera, green juices, and turmeric are all great for healing and soothing the gut.

3. HIT UP YOUR FIBER

One of our body's main methods of eliminating toxins is through your poop! Your body can't do this job properly unless you're getting enough fiber to keep things moving along and sweeping through. Eat plenty of fresh fruit, vegetables, chia, legumes, soaked/activated nuts, quinoa, and brown rice to boost your fiber intake.

4. FEAST ON FERMENTED FOODS

Fermented foods provide the cultured bacteria that our digestive tract needs to function optimally. These products include sauerkraut, kefir, tempeh, miso, kimchi, and yogurt (from pasture-fed, organic sources, and only if you tolerate dairy). Regular consumption of fermented foods can help to keep our microbiome in tip-top condition!

5. EAT SLOWLY

You've probably heard it before, but digestion really does begin in the mouth. Our saliva contains enzymes that start to break down starches in food as we chew. Plus, the act of chewing also signals to our brain that the process of digestion is beginning.[13] The final benefit is that we're less likely to overeat; eating slowly gives our body plenty of time to register that we're full.

6. EAT CALMLY

When we feel stressed, our body switches into fight-or-flight mode. As this happens, our body focuses on the physiological functions that help us to flee or attack an enemy. Blood is diverted to the muscles, our breath rate increases, and our external senses become hyperalert. Simultaneously, systems that are nonessential to fight-or-flight are suppressed—this includes digestion. Therefore, try not to eat when you're feeling stressed and your body isn't in an ideal mode for digestion. If you are stressed and need to eat anyway, taking a few calming, deep breaths before your meal can help.

7. DRINK PLENTY OF WATER

Think of your intestines as one giant tube that propels food along. As this food travels through the tube, nutrients and water are absorbed. However, the body also puts toxins, metabolic by-products, and excess cholesterol back into the tube for elimination. What happens to any tube if the material inside gets hardened? The tube blocks up and transit slows down. Staying hydrated helps to keep materials moving through your digestive "tube" soft and moving freely, thereby supporting the entire absorptive and eliminatory process.

8. MAKE SURE YOU GET DIGESTIVE REST

Our bodies work hard and often need a break; even your digestive system needs rest to work in peak condition. When you think about all the hard (and incredible!) work your digestive system does to transform food into—well, you—it's little wonder that it needs time to repair and heal between meals. Try not to overeat or snack overly often, as this will ensure your belly gets the break that it deserves between all its hard digestive work.

THE POWER OF DETOXIFICATION FOR TRANSFORMATION AND WEIGHT LOSS

In the same way that your body needs a holiday from your work routine, your digestion also needs a break to recharge. Over time, our bodies get run down from not-so-healthy foods, caffeine, alcohol, stress, toxins in our everyday environment, and unhealthy habits that sneak into our daily lives. A cleanse gives our bodies the time, space, and right conditions to restore balance and vitality to themselves once more!

We all want to have glowing and healthy bodies that provide us with an abundance of energy on this journey through life. Within these healthy bodies are the kidneys, liver, skin, colon, and pair of lungs that are fighting against the toxins that we ingest or inhale—toxins from things such as cigarettes, car fumes, carbon emissions, and herbicides/pesticides on the food we eat. Perhaps our bodies are giving us signs that they're running in overdrive and need a pick-me-up. These signs can be disguised in many ways, but here are a few of the telltale signs that we're ready for some TLC.

- Excess stubborn weight that drags you down emotionally and physically
- Low energy throughout the day, especially in the afternoon
- Overeating and feeling like you can't get "full" or satisfied
- Frequent struggles to focus and/or periods of "brain fog"
- Regular constipation and/or loose stools
- Regular bloating and/or excessive flatulence
- Dramatically decreased sex drive
- Sugar cravings throughout the day
- Persistent headaches
- Daily mood swings

HOW CLEANSING CAN HELP WEIGHT LOSS

Feel like you've tried every exercise regime and diet plan under the sun and still can't shift the weight?

It's likely that even if you have tried strict diet plans and counting calories, you may end up back to eating foods that may not serve your body and could potentially cause it harm. Modern society has convinced us that losing weight is simply about calories in, calories out. It's told us that only by exercising more and eating less will we start to see our waistlines shrink.

There's just one problem with this concept: not all calories are created equal. Science has proven that calories from sugar and flour are used completely differently in our bodies than the equal number of calories from leafy greens or nuts. Continued consumption of foods laden with sugar and flour contribute to addictions and overeating through the hormonal triggers from these foods. For example, they can spike insulin and cause inflammation in the body,[14] which can lead to insulin resistance and thus the dreaded belly fat and inability to feel full.[15]

SO HOW WILL A CLEANSE HELP?

If you follow a holistic and natural approach to cleansing, you will be eliminating toxic foods such as processed sugar and flour from your diet. In turn, you will give your body the chance to excrete toxins and balance hormones and brain chemicals that make you hungry and crave nutrient-empty junk foods. Instead of being in a state of nutrient starvation where your body feels the need to store fat, a cleanse with nourishing soups, juices, and smoothies will help your hormones reactivate, thus speeding up your metabolism[16] and turning you into a fat-burning machine.

The recipes in this cookbook have been designed to be naturally cleansing and to support your body's detoxification pathways. If, however, you're looking for a more in-depth juice detox program, you can find out more at foodmatters.com/detox.

EATING FOR BEAUTY AND ANTI-AGING FROM THE INSIDE OUT

Have you been searching for a proven way to look and feel naturally radiant every day? Maybe you've been told by the beauty industry the secret to true beauty lies in some new pill or cream? Well, the truth is our skin, hair, and body crave something completely different.

The little-known truth of natural beauty is that the health of your gut has a direct and immensely powerful effect on the way you look and feel. With 70 percent of our immune system residing in our gut, we need to understand that our skin, hair, and body are a mirror of what's going on inside us.

As experts and renegade researchers in the world of health and wellness, we know that beauty happens from the inside out. This is about helping you to help yourself, using a holistic and natural approach. With ancient, natural, and organic ingredients, you have the power to completely transform the way you look and feel.

11 DAILY HABITS FOR NATURALLY GLOWING SKIN

1. MOVE IT, MOVE IT!

Our skin receives all the healing nutrients it needs through our blood supply. Every time you exercise, you are increasing this beautiful, nourishing blood supply to your skin.[17] You've heard it before and you'll probably hear it again, but it's absolutely vital that we move our body on a daily basis. Your complexion will thank you for it!

2. EAT PLENTY OF HEALTHY FATS

Our skin requires healthy fats to reduce inflammation and build healthy cells. Include plenty of nuts, seeds, avocado, tahini, chia, and cold-pressed oils in your daily diet.[18] And if you aren't vegetarian, bone broth collagen and a couple of servings of fish each week will be helpful too.

3. FIGHT FREE RADICALS WITH ANTIOXIDANTS

Free radicals are a big contributing factor toward aging. You can help to combat their aging action by eating a diet that is rich in antioxidants, meaning plenty of brightly colored fruits and vegetables on your plate each day.[19]

4. "C" REAL BEAUTY BENEFITS

Vitamin C is essential for collagen production. It is the "cement" that keeps our skin supple, firm, and free from wrinkles. Eat plenty of fruit, vegetables, and fresh vegetable juices to get a good daily dose.[20]

5. DON'T PICK ON YOURSELF

While this advice rings true at any time, it is particularly helpful if you experience acne or pimples. Squeezing zits increases the spread of bacteria that exacerbate acne (hence, more acne!) and can also cause scarring. Tempting though it may be, keep your fingers off your face and your breakout is bound to heal faster.

6. SNOOZE MAKEUP-FREE

This habit might be tricky to keep—especially after a late night—but sleeping in your makeup is bad news for your skin. Makeup clogs your pores and if you're using non-organic brands, this also allows extra time for toxic substances to seep into your bloodstream. Cleanse your face before hitting the hay—those extra five minutes are worth it!

7. GIVE GRATITUDE DURING YOUR BEAUTY RITUALS

It can be tempting to find fault and search for flaws in the reflection that gazes back at us. Instead of criticizing your face during daily beauty routines, try to use this time to give thanks for your own unique beauty.

8. GET PLENTY OF SLEEP

There's a reason why it's called beauty sleep. Your body performs all kind of healing, detoxifying, and replenishing work while you're getting your Z's. Research[21] is showing we need more than most people are getting—try for a minimum of eight hours each night!

9. COUNT ON COPPER FOR A VITAL GLOW

Copper plays an important role in collagen synthesis and is also an integral part of the pigment that naturally dyes our eyes, skin, and hair. Eat plenty of copper-rich foods such as seaweed, nuts, legumes, grass-fed organ meats, and cacao to prevent premature aging.[22]

10. BOOST HEALING ZINC

Zinc works 24/7 to heal and repair any damage to your skin. It heals wounds, tidies up tissue injury, and may even help to clear up acne. Consume foods such as pumpkin seeds/pepitas, seafood (wild-caught, sustainable), and cacao to get a regular hit of zinc![23]

11. RESTORE WITH VITAMIN E

Vitamin E is a fat-soluble vitamin that also functions as an antioxidant in the body. It can help to protect your skin against free radicals and sun damage. If your skin is dry or damaged, vitamin E can help to restore nourishment. Good food sources of vitamin E include nuts, seeds, avocado, and oily fish (wild-caught).[24]

BEAUTY-BOOSTING NUTRIENTS

ZINC

Zinc is a mineral that works 24/7 to heal and repair damage in the skin. It's essential for many enzyme reactions and speeds up the biological processes involved in wound healing. Furthermore, zinc can lower the production of free radicals in your skin, which is great news for aging! Excellent food sources of zinc include pumpkin seeds/pepitas, seafood (wild-caught, sustainable), meat (organic, pasture-fed), and cacao.[25]

VITAMIN D

Vitamin D is a fat-soluble vitamin that is converted to its active form by sunlight. It is used widely throughout the body, including the skin, for many functions. It may reduce skin inflammation and influence skin tone.[26] Get vitamin D through safe sun exposure, oily fish (wild-caught), full-cream dairy products (organic, pasture-raised), or supplementation.

OMEGA-3 FATTY ACIDS

These fats are a superfood for the skin! Omega-3 fatty acids can reduce inflammation and nourish the skin at a cellular level. Good sources include oily fish, walnuts, and linseeds/flaxseeds.

VITAMIN E

Vitamin E is a fat-soluble vitamin that also functions as an antioxidant in the body. It can help to protect your skin against free radicals and sun damage. It is also a component of sebum, which helps to moisturize and protect the skin. Food sources include nuts, seeds, avocado, oily fish (wild-caught), and olive oil.[27]

VITAMIN C

Vitamin C is integral for the production of collagen—the stuff that makes your skin stay firm and supple! Vitamin C also protects your skin against free-radical damage and helps to prevent premature aging. Foods that are high in vitamin C include citrus fruits, berries, bell peppers (capsicum), tomatoes, broccoli, kiwi, and superfoods such as goji, acerola, and acai.

COPPER

People with copper deficiency often experience more brittle, wrinkled skin; slower wound healing; higher inflammation; and premature graying. This is because copper plays an important role in collagen synthesis and is part of the pigment that dyes our eyes, skin, and hair. Foods that contain copper include seaweed, nuts, cacao, red wine, organ meats, and legumes.

EATING FIBER FOR BEAUTY

Fiber is a crucial element of food for health. In fact, it's the only "food waste" that we actively seek out, mainly for its vital role in promoting good digestion. Except it's not just digestion that this pseudo nutrient supports; it can be one of the strongest supports for a holistic beauty ritual.

Here's a recap of the different kinds of fibers our bodies need. Soluble fiber dissolves in water or in other digestive tract fluids, which creates a gel that adds bulk to stool. Insoluble fiber attracts water to stool, which makes it easier to pass, placing less strain on the lower organs of the digestive system. Resistant starch is also believed by many to be a "third type of fiber," but it's actually a starch that resists digestive processes in the body and supports the fermentation of fiber for healthy digestion.

But that's all on digestion. How do these fibers help us maintain a naturally beautiful glow? You're about to find out.

HELPS ELIMINATE TOXINS FROM THE BODY

Toxins are ever-present in our modern society, from the food we eat to the air we breathe, and they can have long-lasting effects on our bodies. One of the most common places we find a toxic overload reflected is the skin, manifesting in acne and skin conditions to premature aging. Because of its crucial role in healthy digestion, fiber can help draw out any toxins in the digestive tract and eliminate them as waste.[28]

PROMOTES GUT HEALTH

We now know that gut health is paramount to healthy skin and a healthy body overall, so ensuring gut flora is healthy and thriving should be the cornerstone

of any beauty routine. It often comes down to prebiotic fiber—the kind found in bananas, artichokes, onions, garlic, and whole grains. These ferment in the gut and support the microbiota, in turn promoting health and well-being. Emerging research goes so far as to suggest that prebiotic fibers can have a positive impact on the skin microbiota,[29] which is a significant step in acknowledging the role of holistic beauty.

HELPS TO REDUCE INFLAMMATION IN THE BODY

If there's one thing we've talked about a lot at Food Matters, it's chronic inflammation. Learning to address it isn't a new concept. In fact, it was the focus of physician Max Gerson's signature Gerson Therapy. But lately, it seems as though people are beginning to recognize just how many ways inflammation can impact our health. Chronic inflammation in the body, especially in the digestive tract, tends to show up in the skin in the form of acne and dryness, sometimes even triggering conditions such as psoriasis and eczema. Poor gut health can lead to increased inflammation, so using fiber to address any inflammation can reduce the risk of any skin conditions emerging.

AIDS IN ABSORPTION OF SKIN-SUPPORTING NUTRIENTS

Our skin requires more than just an elaborate beauty routine to thrive; it requires work on the inside too—especially the uptake of various nutrients in the body. One of fiber's key roles, through the slowing of the digestive process, is to help the body absorb essential antioxidants and nutrients found in the diet. Certain nutrients like lutein, lycopene, and vitamin C are needed for healthy skin, so these need to be readily absorbed. Antioxidants are equally important and are known to reduce and prevent aging from oxidative stress.

SLOWS DOWN SIGNS OF AGING

Soluble fiber, the one that dissolves as it moves through the body, is a crucial ingredient to graceful aging. This is because of the slowed digestive process, something we collectively need to get a little better at doing. So when this principle comes to aging, the magic nutrient is collagen. Many of us have come to know it as the holy grail of skincare, keeping complexions soft and supple, as it provides elasticity to the skin barrier. But our body's natural collagen production declines with age, which is why it helps to support its uptake with foods that contain plenty of fiber, as well as the vitamin C essential for absorption.[30]

So, of the fibers—soluble and insoluble, prebiotic or not—what's the best for your skin? Well, it turns out that the answer isn't quite that simple. We need a delicate balance of them all to support our digestion and support our skin in turn. And while there are supplements that offer additional fiber, the best way to absorb it is through our diet. Look to include healthy helpings of fruits and vegetables, as well as organic whole grains, into your daily meals, truly nourishing your skin from the inside out.

IT'S NOT
ALL ABOUT FOOD

Hi, it's Laurentine here. You might remember in Part I when I mentioned returning to Vanuatu, our move to this tropical paradise we now call home. Maybe you're wondering what this has to do with healthy eating and healing. Well, our way of living has completely changed, and I wanted to share why it's not all about food. Yes, what you put in your mouth is fundamental in transforming your health, but how we cope with the daily stressors of life and our mental health is just as important. In this section I wanted to take some time to tell you about our experience, and how our overall well-being can benefit from slowing down and returning to nature, no matter where we reside in the world.

It might sound hard to believe, but this small remote island in the Pacific Ocean called Vanuatu, nestled between Fiji and Australia, feels like home to me. Most people don't know this, but as a young girl, my father took a posting in a bank on a remote island in Vanuatu and subsequently moved our family from Amsterdam to the small island's capital of Port-Vila. To say it was quite a change is an understatement. We literally went overnight from a white Christmas to white sandy beaches, and it was an experience that changed me forever.

Thirty-five years later, I'm back here with my own family, and what I'm learning now about this nation, the people, and the lessons they have for us in the modern world is truly life changing.

RETURNING TO MY ROOTS

In 2017, my father passed away. He suffered a long battle with dementia, and in his final years we visited him often and reminisced about our life growing up in the Pacific. We would pore over photos, artifacts, carvings, and paintings, and tell stories of times gone by.

At the same time, I had two young boys, was running Food Matters with James, and felt like I was having less and less time to spend in nature, connect with my family, and truly approach my mission with peace and a level head.

I felt as though I was running on a treadmill without an off button. Our days consisted of preparing lunches, getting the kids ready for school while trying to get ourselves ready, then into the office for the day, home to scramble a somewhat healthy dinner together, get the kids to bed, clean up, then into work mode with James for the night, and finally off to bed exhausted.

Running a business with your husband is amazing, particularly since some of our best ideas come to us late at night, but it felt like we were mostly always working. Even our international holidays felt like work because we would time them with interviews for the film and then James would mostly be on his phone organizing the next leg of his trip.

I wanted my husband back. I wanted to experience "living in the moment" more. I wanted to see our kids grow up. I wanted us all to spend more time together as a family.

It was a continuous cycle, where sleepless nights started to become the norm, and stress and anxiety were more present in my life than ever before. Something had to give . . .

One day when rummaging through family videos in one of the boxes my father had left behind, I came across old videos of us as kids living in Vanuatu . . . the good old days!

Watching my childhood in those videos ignited something inside me, a craving to go back to my roots. I was drawn to reconnecting with my inner child, to feel young and free again, away from our computers, iPhones, and endless to-do lists. I wanted this for myself, but more so, I wanted this for my children and family.

As a family, we decided to get real and reassess our goals. What beliefs and values did we want? We were ready to evolve as a family.

We put our house in Australia on Airbnb and decluttered our entire life's possessions and realized we didn't need most of it. We moved to Vanuatu with only four suitcases of belongings and three surfboards!

We enrolled Rangi in Vanuatu's international school, which has blown us away with its standards. And we decided to homeschool Hugo because he was only five at the time and we loved the space and the freedom it afforded him.

THE PROFOUND POWER OF SLOWING DOWN

I can tell you, hand on my heart, that there hasn't been a nanosecond of regret. My son Hugo is learning how to open coconuts with a bush knife. James is seeing the old me that he first fell in love with. Rangi has made the most beautiful friendships at the International School. We've got a veggie garden, we swim in the ocean and meditate each morning, and we feel at peace here.

Hugo and Rangi have made the most beautiful friendships, and there truly is a great sense of community. For Hugo's birthday party, we had 20 friends of all ages come over to our house to play old-fashioned birthday games such as the egg-on-a-spoon race and pin the tail on the donkey. I drive at a much slower pace, which you kind of have to since there are no road rules and you are constantly dodging potholes! Rangi has fallen in love with horse riding in the local riders club in Bellevue. Hugo has learned how to snorkel and goes searching for Nemo fish and colorful sea stars on the reef whenever we take him to the beach.

I have a fresh coconut for breakfast each morning, and papayas, limes, avocados, and local sweet potatoes are high on the list in every market trip. James gets to end the day paddling out at his local surf spot before enjoying a shell of kava in the local "pub"/kava bar on the beach.

The challenges will no doubt continue to arise—like yesterday, when I had to take a cold shower because we ran out of gas and the only way to replace it was to physically drive to the gas station and replace the gas container. But I now enjoy the zen of a cold-water shower. And James is often heard cursing the local internet

provider because just when we have an important live call, it always seems to drop out! And it is hard not being close to our family back in Australia and whom we miss dearly. But, for the record, I do feel like we have family here in Vanuatu. Every person we pass on our road greets us, and neighbors come to drop off excess vegetables and bananas from their forest gardens. I've never felt more of a sense of community!

ONE OF THE HAPPIEST PLACES ON EARTH

Deciding to live somewhere that consistently ranks high as being one of the happiest places on Earth has helped us to also partake in some of that happiness! It's not just the "chill vibe" you pick up on that has that effect. It's the love and passion from the local island people. You get to be more present in the *being* rather than *doing*. Vanuatu has been quite healing for me—walking barefoot, eating the local food and bush medicine, reconnecting with my beautiful family, and becoming a much more grounded version of myself. And, of course, we've been able to take all this amazing local knowledge back to the kitchen—and now, we're sharing it with you.

To see how we incorporated local flavors and tropical fruits and vegetables from the island into our Food Matters recipes, check out Laurentine's Island Breakfast Bowl (page 125) and James's Green Papaya Salad (page 255).

PREPARING YOUR KITCHEN

Regain your confidence in the kitchen and take the fear out of cooking by setting yourself up with the tools and ingredients you need.

HOW TO HEALTHIFY YOUR KITCHEN
BUY MORE OF THIS

LEAFY GREENS
Bitter Greens
Collard Greens
Chard
Beet Greens
Arugula
Lettuce
Kale
Spinach
Silverbeet
Bok Choy

VEGETABLES
Celery
Sprouts
Cucumber
Broccoli
Cauliflower
Brussels Sprouts
Cabbage
Carrot
Asparagus
Mushrooms
Garlic
Leek
Green Beans
Onion
Radish
Fennel
Zucchini
Peas
Seaweed
Vegetable Juice

LOW-SUGAR FRUIT
Berries
Avocado
Lemon
Grapefruit
Lime
Olives

HEALING HERBS & SPICES
Turmeric
Ginger
Fresh Herbs
Herbal Teas

PROBIOTIC-RICH FOODS
Sauerkraut & Cultured Vegetables
Apple Cider Vinegar (with the Mother)
Coconut Kefir
Coconut Yogurt

FRESH FRUIT
Apples
Plums
Oranges
Peaches
Pears
Cherries
Kiwi Fruit
Pomegranate
Melons
Grapes
Mangos
Figs
Pineapple
Banana
Papaya
Passionfruit

ROOT VEGETABLES
Parsnips
Yams
Sweet Potato
Pumpkin & Squash
Beetroot

NIGHTSHADES
Tomatoes
Eggplant
Peppers
Potatoes

NUTS & SEEDS
Almonds
Brazil Nuts
Pecans
Cashews
Sunflower Seeds
Pepitas
Sesame Seeds
Chia Seeds
Hemp Seeds
Flaxseeds
Nut Milk
Nut Butters
*Ideally nuts & seeds should be activated.

GLUTEN-FREE GRAINS
Quinoa
Millet
Buckwheat
Amaranth
Rice
Oats

LEGUMES
Lentils
Garbanzo Beans
Fava Beans
Kidney Beans
Black Peas
Pinto Beans
Navy Beans
*Ideally legumes should be soaked.

SUPERMARKET SHOPPING GUIDE

BUY LESS OF THAT

WILD SEAFOOD
Sardines
Herring
Salmon
Mahi Mahi
Oysters
Mussels
Scallops
Clams
Shrimp

COLD-PRESSED OILS
Coconut Oil
Olive Oil
Flaxseed Oil
Macadamia Oil
Hemp Oil

**FERMENTED DAIRY
PRODUCTS**
Yogurt
Kefir
Buttermilk
Cultured Butter

SOY PRODUCTS
Tempeh
Tofu
Natto

EGGS

CACAO

COFFEE

WHOLE-GRAIN PRODUCTS
Rice Pasta
Sprouted Grains
Sourdough

DAIRY PRODUCTS
Butter
Ghee
Milk

MEATS
Chicken
Turkey
Duck
Beef
Pork
Lamb
Goat

†Ideally all meat &
dairy products should
be pasture-raised &
grass-fed.

**REFINED GRAIN
PRODUCTS**
White Bread
Pastries
White Crackers
Pizza
Pasta & Noodles
Breakfast Cereal

**PROCESSED MEATS &
CHEESES**
Deli Meats
Sausages
Hot Dogs
Bacon
Jerky
Canned Meats
Cheese

HIGH-SUGAR PRODUCTS
Soda
Energy Drinks
Iced Tea
Sweet Cereal
Candy
Conventional
Chocolate
Cordial
Packaged Fruit
Juice
Flavored Milks
Premade Salad
Dressings

TRANS FATS
Deep-Fried Foods
Donuts
Chips

REFINED SEED OILS
Canola Oil
Soybean Oil
Cottonseed Oil
Vegtable Oil
Margarine &
Spreadable Butter
Rice Bran Oil

ALCOHOL

FOOD STORAGE 101

Any foodie will tell you that the key to a kitchen is a handful of simple routines, or "hacks." How you store your food is just as important as the food you buy itself. Whether you're making the most out of shelf life, looking to reduce waste, or trying to save time and space, there's a few simple rules to follow.

ROOT VEGETABLES

The pantry is one of the best places to store root vegetables. You can also put them in the cooler, in darker corners, in storage baskets and canvas bags, or you can use large ceramic vessels to store things such as potatoes, pumpkins, and onions. This will prevent them from sprouting or getting too weathered by harsh environments.

FRESH HERBS

When dealing with fresh herbs, here are a few ways to prevent them from going limp and sad looking. The easiest way is to fill a glass jar or tumbler partway with cold water and place the herbs in there like a bouquet of flowers so that the roots and stems are submerged in water. Then wrap the leaves in reusable plastic (we like to reuse sandwich bags) and store them in the refrigerator. Alternatively, you can lightly spritz the herbs with water or roll them in a damp paper towel, then store them in your vegetable crisper drawer.

GREEN LEAFY VEGETABLES

To keep salad leaves fresh, you can use the same wet paper towel hack that you would with herbs, or you can keep them ready to go at a moment's notice. One of the best kitchen gadgets is a compact salad spinner. The ventilated basket stops any produce from going limp or rotten too quick, and whenever it needs a freshen up or wash, you can rinse and spin with a fuss-free approach. Plus, the sealed lid keeps your greens fresher for longer and they're ready to put on the table at dinnertime.

FISH

Make sure foods such as fish get your attention as soon as you get home. It's always wise to take a chiller bag to the store if possible and get it straight into the fridge when you get home. Portion the fish into the different serving sizes you'll need throughout the week, and if you're not eating it the next day, wrap the servings individually and freeze them for when you need them next. Make sure to take the portion of fish out of the freezer the night before you need to use it and place it in the refrigerator to defrost at the perfect pace.

MUSHROOMS

Most of your food should be stored in individual containers or the vegetable crisper, but there's an exception to the rule. Mushrooms last better when kept in a brown paper bag. Don't put them in the crisper drawer either, but rather the shelf just above. This will ensure the mushrooms have the right climate to stay fresher for longer.

PRODUCE PREPARATION

It's easy enough after your weekly trip to the market or grocer to get home and shove your produce in the fridge wherever there is space. But by dedicating an extra 15 minutes to rotating your fridge contents and getting the new fruits and vegetables ready for the week ahead, you'll thank yourself infinitely when it comes to dinners throughout the busy week. Start by pulling out any leftover produce from last week. Then, take your fresh foods and wash, chop, and prep them if need be before putting them in containers to be on hand for the week ahead. Once they're good to go, make sure your older produce is still okay to eat (compost if not) and place it back on top—this means you'll reach for the food that needs using first.

GLASS CONTAINERS AND REUSABLE JARS

Speaking of containers, making sure you have ample containers is the key to keeping your fridge organized. They can be a relatively inexpensive set, but they'll make your life easier. Glass or ceramic containers that can stack on each other are the gold standard, as you can be sure no chemicals in the plastic are leaching into your food while also making the most of space—plus they're much sturdier and are great for storing leftovers too. Alternatively, any reusable jars always make great containers for foods such as quinoa or individual leftover portions of soup.

REUSABLE FOOD COVERS

If you're looking for ways to make your kitchen more sustainable, consider switching out your cling wrap for a washable, reusable alternative. Silicone food covers and beeswax wraps are readily available online, and, while they're initially more expensive, they last forever, so they will save you money in the long run! And if you're crafty or creative, you can easily make your own beeswax wraps at home with your favorite fabrics.

FREEZING FOOD

When making food in bulk or deciding to freeze any leftovers, place the food in smaller containers to freeze in individual portions. That way, you only have to defrost what you need each time. You can use kitchen tools such as muffin tins to freeze big batches of pesto for smaller servings or ice cube trays to freeze single-serve portions of lemon juice. Also, try to keep food in like spaces—leftovers in one section, meats in another, fruits for smoothies in one area, and sweet treats somewhere else. It'll make it that much easier when trying to find what you need (and remembering to get more when you run out).

CUT THE END OF
THE STEMS OF
YOUR HERBS, THEN
PUT THEM IN CUPS
OF WATER ON YOUR
COUNTER.

KEEP YOUR
JARS! (USE FOR
STORAGE)

DITCH THE TAKE-
AWAY COFFEE
CUPS-BRING A
REUSABLE ONE!

SALAD GREENS
CAN BE WRAPPED
IN TEA TOWELS
OR DAMP CLOTHS
AND KEPT IN THE
FRIDGE TO LAST
LONGER.

SUSTAINABLE
KITCHEN
SWAPS

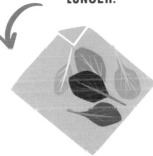

STAND CELERY AND
CARROTS IN JARS
WITH WATER.

PUT LEFTOVERS
IN JARS.

BRING YOUR OWN
REUSABLE BAGS
TO THE STORE!

STORE ONIONS +
POTATOES IN A DARK
CUPBOARD.

COMPOST

WRAP BEANS AND
PEAS IN A DAMP
CLOTH TO LAST
LONGER.

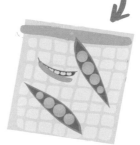

WRAP BREAD IN A CLOTH
OR PILLOWCASE AND STORE
IT IN A WOODEN BIN.

SWITCH TO BEES-
WAX WRAPS!

METAL + GLASS CON-
TAINERS ARE GREAT
FOR STORAGE OR
LUNCH ON THE GO.

BUILDING A NOURISHING PANTRY

We believe the secret to a healthy, well-stocked kitchen is pantry staples. Staples that make a recipe sing, that are always on call, and that can be used in just about everything. These ingredients are just as tasty as they are versatile, whether they are used in soups and curries or smoothie bowls and salads. And they're brimming with health benefits too!

1. EXTRA VIRGIN OLIVE OIL

Although extra virgin olive oil has a lower smoking point than some other cooking oils, it is perfect for cooking at a lower heat and using in all the best dressings. Extra virgin olive oil (especially cold-pressed and organic where possible) is the highest quality available, retaining more of the natural vitamins and minerals than other presses. Essentially, it's unrefined, so it's not treated with chemicals or altered with temperatures. Olive oil is a great source of healthy monounsaturated fats, which help control cholesterol levels and have been linked with heart health.[1] Drizzle it on steamed veggies or onto a nice cold salad. Extra virgin olive oil is good for low-heat sautéing. However, at temperatures above 200 degrees, it can oxidize, which may not be good for your body. For cooking at a higher temperature, we use coconut oil or a dash of sesame oil.

2. MAPLE SYRUP, DATES, AND HONEY

Life is certainly a little sweeter with sugar. However, the levels of sugar that our society is consuming are a direct reflection of our global chronic health concerns. But doing away with sweet flavors altogether doesn't have to be an option. Our picks for the best natural sweeteners to use are maple syrup, dates, honey, and coconut sugar. While these options are still to be consumed in moderation, they are from natural sources and are high in micronutrients when compared with refined white sugar. It can take some getting used to, but our recipes will help guide you into an easy and delicious transition!

3. UNREFINED SEA SALT FLAKES

While we're cautious with our sodium intake, we know that a little salt is important for both our health and making meals taste delicious, so when we need to, we opt for unrefined sea salt flakes. What makes salt "bad" is the process of refining, which includes chemical production and bleaching, a process that robs the food of its naturally occurring nutrients. Unrefined salt, on the other hand, is actually full of essential minerals and nutrients for proper electrolyte balance.

4. HARISSA

Made from blended red chilis, garlic, olive oil, and vinegar, harissa originates from Tunisia and packs a punch of flavor that can easily elevate any dish. These days you can find the paste in most commercial supermarkets, either in the international aisle or among the spices. If you can't find harissa, it can be whipped up quickly by simply adding the aforementioned ingredients into a food processor. Our favorite way to use harissa is as a marinade for fish or other proteins, mixed with extra virgin olive oil and lemon to create a dressing, or by adding it to curries, tagines, and stews for flavor.

5. PURE VANILLA EXTRACT

Derived from an edible tropical orchid plant and used for hundreds of years across the globe, vanilla is known for more than just its universally loved flavor. Vanilla has proven aphrodisiac ability, is valued as an antidepressant and anti-inflammatory, and can have a relaxing and calming general effect.[2] We love adding pure vanilla extract to sweeter dishes like poached pears, granolas, and smoothies.

6. HEMP SEEDS

Hemp is one of the most resourceful, sustainable plants on our planet right now. It's used in everything from oils and flours to clothing and bed linen, and it's a staple in our kitchen. Hemp seeds are rich in healthy fats and essential fatty acids, providing a good source of omegas, which we know are vital for brain health, among many other things. They are also a great protein source and contain high amounts of vitamin E, phosphorus, potassium, sodium, magnesium, sulfur, calcium, iron, and zinc, but take care, you'll want to remember to keep them in the fridge to help retain all of their beautiful benefits.[3] If you're looking for an easy way to slip them into meals, try sprinkling a tablespoon on your salad.

7. HULLED TAHINI

You may be surprised to know that tahini is made from ground sesame seeds. This deliciously nutty paste is an essential ingredient in a wide variety of food, from dressings to gluten-free brownies. The best part? It's actually good for you. Tahini contains more protein than milk and most nuts. It's a rich source of the B vitamins that boost energy and brain function; vitamin E, which is protective against heart disease and stroke; and important minerals such as magnesium, iron, and calcium.[4] We often opt for the hulled version for its slightly sweet and muted flavor.

8. APPLE CIDER VINEGAR

This is one of our favorite kinds of vinegar to use. The tangy flavored liquid aids in digestion and can even be used in place of lemon water. ACV has widespread health properties, including antimicrobial and antioxidant effects. What's more, evidence suggests it may aid weight loss, reduce cholesterol, lower blood sugar levels, and improve the symptoms of diabetes.[5] ACV adds pizazz to salads as part of a perfectly easy dressing, and it can even be used with a bit of baking soda to help make vegan treats rise. Just when you think you've seen it all, it's also good as a surface cleaner when diluted in water.

9. TAMARI

While soy sauce is derived from GMO ingredients and is packed with wheat, tamari—the ultimate alternative—is a traditional, wheat-free version that makes a regular appearance in Food Matters meals. If you have a gluten intolerance, take care to check the labels. Because of increased demand, major manufacturers have been searching for ways to bulk out this normally gluten-free alternative.

10. SAUERKRAUT

We usually make our own sauerkraut because it's that easy, delicious, and nutritious, but many store-bought varieties pack just the same punch. During the fermentation process, beneficial probiotics, or "live bacteria," are produced, and these probiotics are what give sauerkraut most of its health benefits. It provides probiotics and vitamin K_2 and may help you strengthen your immune system, improve your digestion, reduce your risk of certain diseases, and lose weight.

11. PALEO MAYONNAISE OR VEGAN MAYONNAISE

This is a favorite addition to almost any dish. Whether we're making vegan burgers or a poke bowl, paleo or vegan mayo adds extra creamy, healthy fats. Mayonnaise, when made traditionally, is a mix of egg, oil, and either vinegar or lemon juice. One of the best vegan alternatives is using aquafaba, the brine from a can of chickpeas, in the place of an egg. Our insider tip: mix in a little crushed garlic for an easy aioli.

With a pantry full of good-quality and versatile ingredients, you're setting your kitchen up for success. A few key staples alongside fresh, organic produce and a handful of good recipes are all you really need. Now you just need the inspiration to use them—but don't worry, that's coming.

HEALING HERBS AND SPICES EVERY KITCHEN SHOULD HAVE

With herbs and spices being the key to healing for thousands of years, which healing spices are best kept close at hand in your kitchen?! Here is our list of the top healing spices you should keep well stocked at home.

1. TURMERIC
Turmeric can help reduce inflammation and the risk of arthritis, Alzheimer's, and heart disease.[6] One study[7] in healthy middle aged volunteers showed that taking 80 milligrams of curcumin, a component of turmeric, once a day for four weeks reduced markers of inflammation and oxidative stress.
How to use it
This earthy and slightly bitter spice is a flavorful addition to teas, juices, and smoothies. It is best used in a healing nut milk latte, as a dip that you can put on

practically anything, and in scrambled eggs, one of our personal favorites.

2. CUMIN
Cumin is a slightly sweet, nutty, and warming spice that can help you lose weight and increase your metabolism. It also aids in relieving congestion and indigestion.[8]
How to use it
You can purchase cumin as a powder, but we love buying cumin seeds whole and grinding them in a mortar and pestle. There's something wonderful about smelling freshly ground cumin and knowing how much good it will do for your body when you consume it. Cumin is a staple in most curries and Indian dishes but is also great in scrambled eggs and healing teas.

3. CAYENNE
Made from cayenne pepper, cayenne is fiery hot spice that has been used medicinally for thousands of years. The key component in this spice, capsaicin, is known to help boost metabolism, lower blood pressure by relaxing the vessels, and help prevent osteoarthritis.[9]
How to use it
Though you can purchase capsaicin creams, it's much easier to add a sprinkle of cayenne to your food to receive the benefits. Because this is such a powerful spice, it doesn't take much!

4. PAPRIKA
Paprika is a pepper-based spice that helps fight a range of diseases due largely to its ability to fight oxidative stress. Paprika helps reduce inflammation and may help prevent and fight autoimmune conditions and some cancers.[10]

How to use it

Paprika is an earthy, sweet, and peppery spice, most popularly known as a key ingredient in Hungary's signature dish, goulash. We also love to use paprika in many of our dishes, such as Spinach & Harissa Shakshuka (page 122), Naked Burrito Bowl (page 143), and Crunchy Cauliflower Tacos (page 182).

5. GARLIC

Despite the garlic breath it can create, garlic is an antioxidant, antibiotic, and an aphrodisiac. Garlic boosts the immune system and can help destroy free radicals and help prevent heart disease by reducing atherosclerosis, or hardening of the arteries; lowering cholesterol; and lowering blood pressure.[11]

How to use it

To receive the full spectrum of health benefits, after you chop or crush it, leave your garlic to sit for five minutes before cooking or eating to allow the health-promoting allicin to form. Garlic can be eaten raw or cooked in a variety of ways, from including it in stir-fries or in mashed potatoes to roasting it and eating it whole. We particularly love making tahini garlic sauce for falafels.

6. BLACK PEPPER

More than just a basic flavoring to any meal, black pepper is an antioxidant with antidepressant properties, antimicrobial potential,[12] and gastro-protective modules. Additionally, black pepper activates free-radical scavenging and is also thought to be helpful in chemoprevention and controlling the progression of tumor growth.[13] As if that wasn't enough, black pepper is also attributed to improving cognitive brain and gastrointestinal functionality and boosting nutrient absorption.

How to use it

Black pepper is complementary to most savory dishes, where a pinch can be used to finish the dish. We incorporate pepper into our dips, dressings, salads, snacks, and dinners, preferring freshly ground black peppercorns.

7. GINGER

In Ayurvedic medicine, ginger is known as a "natural medicine chest" because of its time-tested digestion-friendly and anti-inflammatory properties,[14] as well as its ability to help improve the absorption of essential nutrients in the body, clear sinuses and congestion, relieve nausea, and assist with reducing joint pain.

How to use it

With its pungent and spicy flavor, ginger can be enjoyed in a multitude of ways, from tea to juice to baked goods, and from pickled meal accompaniments to sweet treats to stir-fries. We find drinking ginger with water or in a juice is a great way to start each day.

8. CINNAMON

Cinnamon is a sweet spice you can enjoy guilt-free as it is a powerful antioxidant and can have a positive effect on your blood sugar levels, digestion, and immune system, as well as blood cholesterol. When taken in strong doses, cinnamon has been known to help reduce the risk of diabetes, cancer, and neurodegenerative diseases.[15]

How to use it

Cinnamon can be enjoyed with sweet and savory dishes as well as in hot and cold beverages. You will find it used in many of our recipes, from sweet smoothies to our Creamy Cinnamon & Apple Oatmeal (page 118) to the Moroccan Vegetable Tagine (page 162).

9. CLOVES

Cloves are known for curing cold natured problems that affect the central nervous system, as well as aiding digestion by increasing heat in the stomach and liver.[16] Consuming cloves can aid in functions of the throat and speech, and, strangely enough, cloves can help reduce hiccups!

How to use it

For the hiccup cure, warm a few cloves in a spoonful of butter or ghee and drink it. For other ailments, or to enjoy the strong flavor notes, try adding cloves to smoothies or hot chocolate.

10. NUTMEG

Nutmeg has been used for centuries to help alleviate pain, gastrointestinal disorders, and skin wounds and infections, with the added benefit of having a calming effect.[17] It's also been reported as an aphrodisiac. Caution must be taken when consuming nutmeg, however, as consuming excessive amounts can lead to unpleasant hallucinogenic effects.[18]

How to use it

You only need a sprinkle of ground nutmeg, as this spice is very flavorsome. Nutmeg is often used in festive baking and eggnog drinks, and it can also be used to spice up fruits and vegetables, either in food or beverages.

THE BENEFITS OF SOAKING AND ACTIVATING NUTS AND SEEDS

You will notice throughout the book that we suggest using activated nuts and seeds in our recipes. Nuts and seeds are very nutritious and high on the list of foods to include in your diet. The trouble is, your body may not be getting the full nutritional potential of the nuts and seeds. Soaking and activating your nuts and seeds stimulates the early germination and sprouting process within the nut and seed. This has a twofold benefit. First, enzyme inhibitors are disarmed so that the plant can begin its next stage of growth. Second, phytic acid levels drop as the nut taps into this energy store in preparation for its impending growth spurt. We end up with a delicious, nutritious snack that our bodies can more easily digest and absorb!

While you can buy activated nuts and seeds from health food stores, they do tend to be a bit pricey. As an easy alternative, you can create your own at home! Here's how:

1. Pour 2 cups of your favorite nuts and seeds into a large bowl (it's worthwhile making a larger batch in one go).

2. Cover your nuts with filtered water mixed with sea salt (most nuts need approximately 2 teaspoons salt).

3. Make sure your nuts are completely submerged in the salt water, with an inch or two on top to spare. The nuts will absorb water as they soak and may grow mold if not kept submerged in water.

4. Most nuts and seeds should be soaked for 7 to 12 hours, although almonds need a little longer at 12 to 14 hours.

5. After soaking, strain the excess water.

6. Place nuts on baking trays or dehydrator racks if you are using a dehydrator.

7. Slowly roast at very low heat (150°F/65°C) in an oven or dehydrator for 12 to 24 hours.

8. The nuts are ready when they are completely dried out (do they pass the crunch test when you bite into them?). The nuts will spoil easily and become moldy if they are not fully dry.

9. Store your delicious, activated nuts and seeds in an airtight container in the pantry for up to three months.

THE BEST OILS FOR COOKING

Fat and oil have had a pretty bad rap over the years. The "fat-free" '80s led to the demise of these once revered staples, which has only been intensified with highly processed and refined vegetable oils and trans fats increasingly permeating our modern foods. Despite what you may have been told, oils are an essential part of cooking in every kitchen and not all of them are unhealthy.

Choosing the best oils to cook with doesn't need to be daunting; it simply comes down to a two-step approach. First, is the oil or fat in its nutritious raw form and suitable for human consumption in small amounts? And second, does the oil have a high smoke point, in that it can resist high temperatures before oxidizing, which can create harmful free radicals?

With that in mind, here are a few cooking oils that we love.

1. COCONUT OIL

Coconut oil is one of the best additions to any whole-foods pantry. The largest portion of fat in coconut oil comes from a healthy saturated fat called lauric acid, which has been proven to encourage your body to burn fat and raise HDL (good) cholesterol in your blood, which may help reduce heart disease risk.[19] When it comes to cooking, coconut oil is resistant to oxidizing at high temperatures, which makes it a great stable oil for cooking. Plus, its delightfully fragrant flavor makes it ideal for many Asian-inspired dishes.

2. EXTRA VIRGIN OLIVE OIL

No kitchen is complete without cold pressed extra virgin olive oil. But what sets this apart from your regular olive oil? It's that the first extraction from the olive is done without any heat or chemicals that destroy its integrity. Extra virgin olive oil has widespread health benefits, including improving heart health, promoting brain function, and having potential anti-cancer benefits.[20] It can also handle moderately high temperatures without oxidizing.

3. GRASS-FED BUTTER

Unlike milk, butter has very low amounts of lactose, the protein in milk to which many people react. So if you don't react well to milk, you may still do okay with butter. This has to do with how butter is made. And if you choose to include small amounts of dairy in your diet, good-quality, organic, grass-fed butter is a good option. We also occasionally use both butter and olive oil when cooking, as this can help to avoid the butter from burning. Studies have shown that grass-fed dairy is a richer source than non-grass-fed for vitamin A, omega-3 fatty acids, and up to 500 percent more conjugated linoleic acid (CLA), which is linked to promising anti-cancer effects and vitamin K_2.[21] It's still a concentrated source of fats and calories, so it's important to make sure you're not smothering your dishes in it.

4. GRASS-FED GHEE

Ghee is the holy grail of dairy products. It is a form of highly clarified butter that has traditionally been used in Indian cooking and Ayurveda. The process of converting butter to ghee involves melting it to remove the milk solids, resulting in significantly fewer dairy sugars and proteins. This simple change in form may make it a great alternative for anyone navigating a dairy intolerance or lactose sensitivity. Unlike butter, ghee won't turn rancid at room temperature and retains its original flavor and freshness for up to a year. While other fats and oils can slow down the body's digestive process and give us that heavy feeling in our stomach, ghee stimulates the digestive system by encouraging the secretion of stomach acids to break down food.[22] Ghee is one of our must-reach-for cooking essentials, because of both its nutty flavor and high burning temperature.

WHAT'S THE BEST GLUTEN-FREE FLOUR FOR COOKING?

It's estimated that 1 percent of the global population has celiac disease, with another 7 percent having some form of gluten sensitivity.[23] And this number is on the rise.

Gluten sensitivity, or even excessive consumption of gluten (like we have in the modern Western diet), can contribute to cascading cases of inflammation, autoimmune disease, and chronic health conditions.[24] Autoimmune disease can have a long-term impact on your health if not treated carefully, including increasing your risk of heart disease, cancer, and gut inflammation.[25]

One thing we have realized is that it's not only the gluten that's contributing to chronic health concerns; it's also the farming process. Monocropping (the practice of growing a single crop year after year on the same land), especially wheat, can have devastating impacts on your health due to the increasing amounts of pesticides and chemicals used.

And if you're reaching for a gluten-free blend on your grocer's shelf, more often than not you'll find it packed with chemically made preservatives, thickeners, stabilizers, and colors to help it mimic the texture of wheat. So where you can, make sure to buy organic gluten-free flours with the least ingredients possible. When starting out with gluten-free baking and cooking, much of the texture and taste issues are directly related to the types of flours used. Luckily, over the years, we've tried nearly every gluten-free flour imaginable, and here are three of the best that we recommend.

MANIOC/CASSAVA FLOUR

This root vegetable blend is one of the closest textures you'll find to "the real deal." Normally, multiple flours and additives are blended to achieve a gluten-like texture, but that's not the case with cassava. The flour (derived from the starchy tuber) has high carbohydrate content, making it a valuable food in many indigenous cultures. Unlike other alternatives, cassava flour is very mild and neutral in flavor, as well as low in both fat and sugar. It's also not grainy or gritty in texture—rather, it's soft and powdery. Plus, the blend is great for everyone as it is free of gluten, grain, and nuts!

TAPIOCA FLOUR

From time to time, the terms *cassava flour* and *tapioca flour* are used interchangeably. However, there are some very important differences to note. Tapioca is a starch extracted from the cassava root through a process of washing and pulping. The wet pulp is then squeezed to extract a starchy liquid. Once all the water evaporates from the starchy liquid, the tapioca flour remains.

Tapioca is an almost pure starch, meaning it possesses similar binding properties to gluten. It contains small amounts of protein, fat, and fiber but still has a valuable role in digestion. It is a source of resistant starch, which, as the name implies, makes it resistant to certain functions in the digestive system. This kind of starch is linked to benefits such as feeding the friendly bacteria in the gut, thereby reducing gut inflammation and harmful bacteria, and lowering blood sugar levels.[26]

ALMOND MEAL

If nuts are still a mainstay in your diet, almond meal is another great substitute for plain wheat flour—especially when it comes to baking. It has a sweet, buttery, and slightly nutty flavor, with a texture perfect for cakes and crumbles. It is also one of the most nutritious flour substitutes, as it is high in protein, manganese, vitamin E, and monounsaturated fats; low in carbohydrates; and contains fiber. Plus, it's relatively easy to make from the leftover pulp of homemade almond milk.

OUR FAVORITE KITCHEN TOOLS

Whether you're an avid cook or just a beginner, there are some tools you need to equip your kitchen with to get the most out of cooking. Every whole-foods kitchen can be easily equipped with the right tools to make your own healthy "fast food." Here are our essential kitchen tools to make healthy cooking easier.

BLENDER

If you thought blenders were just for smoothies, please think again! A good-quality, multifunctional blender will create items as varied as nut butter and freshly milled flour. Blenders are also the ultimate home "fast food" appliance. You can whizz together a vitalizing breakfast smoothie or delicious raw veggie soup for dinner in less time than it takes to start the car! Before you invest in a blender, consider what you are most likely to use it for. A small, one-cup model such as a NutriBullet is perfect for individual smoothies and veggie soups on the run. If you're feeding a family and can utilize some more advanced features such as flour milling, we recommend a high-powered, multifunctional option such as a Vitamix. For the recipes in this book, a standard blender will work perfectly.

FOOD PROCESSOR

If you're not too confident with your knife skills or simply don't enjoy laboring over the chopping board, a food processor will change your life. This appliance is like having your own personal sous-chef to prep your food. It will revolutionize your approach to cooking and save you so much time in making healthy meals.

A good-quality food processor will slice, shred, chop, or puree just about any food you can imagine. A great food processor will chop your fruit and veggies, slice salad ingredients, puree baby food, make nut milk, and even knead your dough. Salads and stir-fries are unbelievably quick and easy when you take out chopping time! Simply wash your produce, remove unwanted skins and seeds, and let your food processor take care of the rest.

JUICER

A daily juice is your 15-minute nutrient express to vibrant health. It delivers vitalizing nutrients into each cell and primes your body to work well for the day. With roughly 90 percent of Americans not eating enough fruit and veggies,[27] juicing is one of the easiest ways to boost your intake.

Juicing extracts the nutrients from your produce and concentrates these vitamins and minerals into one convenient glass. We highly recommend a good-quality, cold-pressed model and personally use the Hurom juicer. The Hurom gently extracts maximum nutrients while maintaining the enzyme quality of your juice. The easy-clean system of the Hurom makes tidying up no-fuss and is a great time-saving feature.

This means that you are getting a high-yield, nutritious juice that can last in the fridge for up to 24 hours, saving the need to prepare a juice fresh daily and cutting down time in the kitchen. A juicer requires no cooking skills and is something anyone can use, no matter how confident you are in the kitchen.

KNIFE SET

If you cook on a regular basis, you already understand the frustration of using a blunt, inefficient knife. When your blades are poor quality, the knife edge slips easily (dangerously close to fingers!), bruises fresh produce, and inhibits how fast you can cut your food. By contrast, when you have a sharp, high-quality knife set at your fingertips, cooking becomes faster, more convenient, and a whole lot less stressful. A chef's knife will be the most versatile choice; we love using a Japanese or German style. Look for something lighter in weight with a thin blade, and be sure to ask if you can test it in the store.

SPIRALIZER

This is one handy kitchen tool that kids big and small absolutely *love*! Spiralizers transform basic vegetables into fantastic, squiggly spirals that make healthy spaghetti or noodle substitutes. Also, the spirals look simply stunning in salads and stir-fries!

Spiralizers are cheap, easy to use, and a brilliant asset toward building your veggie intake. Most models are very safe and can be used as a kitchen activity the little ones will adore.

Large, stand-alone models typically come with various attachments to make "spirals" of different shapes and sizes, ideal for making larger meals to feed a crowd in a hurry. Alternatively, you can also purchase smaller, handheld spiralizers. These are better suited for making a small quantity but may only have one "spiral" design option.

OUR FAVORITE POTS AND PANS

Working with food all day long, we've realized that it's not just what we're putting on our plate that matters—it's what we're using to cook our meals too. Over the years there have been some remarkable shifts in food technology, especially with the development of nonstick cookware. At first, it felt like a game changer—no need for excess oils and butter, right? But with time we realized that a lot of this cookware was having a profound impact on our health, through surface compounds that came to be known as carcinogens.

Unfortunately, Teflon has become a very common coating on pots and pans. This coating is very toxic, inviting off-gases and toxic chemicals into our home environment and, more alarmingly, into our food. New technologies continue to pop up, but are they the safest choices for our family?

We've got our tried-and-true kitchen essentials, and these are the pans we swear by.

CAST IRON

Number one on our list time and time again is a good cast-iron pan. They're easy to come by, but the best part is that they're nothing fancy—cast iron has been used for centuries. And if you look after cast-iron pans, they'll last that long too! Clean your cast iron by rinsing with warm water and a small amount of soap only as needed; for a really dirty pan, scrub with salt and a little oil, then wipe clean. From the stovetop to the oven, and fires if you dare, this is the one pan that every kitchen needs.

STAINLESS STEEL

Depending on what's for dinner, stainless steel cookware can often be nonstick. They're best used at lower temperatures to ensure the longevity of the pans, and, like their cast-iron cousin, there are no hidden chemicals lurking below the surface. Just simple, healthy cookware at its finest.

PART
4
RECIPES

JUICES

Each recipe here makes one 2-cup serving and takes just 5 minutes to prep. For each recipe, juice all the ingredients together and enjoy straight away!

SUPER DETOX GREEN JUICE

Cucumber and celery are incredible for hydration first thing in the morning, as the mineral balance in these vegetables means that your cells can absorb more water. The celery leaves can make the juice bitter, which is why we recommend removing them for a milder taste.

½ bunch celery, leaves removed

2 small cucumbers (or 1 large)

1 lime, peeled

2 inches of fresh ginger root, peeled

1 pear or apple (optional)

SUPREME DIGEST GREEN JUICE

The combination of fennel, mint, and ginger helps to soothe the digestive system and reduce inflammation. Fennel has a long history of being used to treat a variety of gut and digestive problems, including stomach aches, flatulence, diarrhea, and constipation.

½ bunch celery, leaves removed

2 small cucumbers (or 1 large)

½ fennel bulb

½ bunch mint

1 lime, peeled

2 inches of fresh ginger root, peeled

1 apple or pear (optional)

GREEN HYDRATOR

Coconut water is a great addition to green juice because it's packed with beneficial electrolytes including sodium, potassium, calcium, magnesium, and phosphorus. These electrolytes help the cells in our body uptake water and boost hydration. It's believed that the electrolyte content is so similar to human blood that it was used during World War II as a plasma replacement for wounded soldiers.

3 small cucumbers	1 lime, peeled
1 cup coconut water	1 apple or pear (optional)
1 cup spinach	
½ bunch mint	

PURIFYING JUICE

Beetroot juice is an incredible blood cleanser or purifier. This is because of its antioxidant and detoxification properties. Consuming beetroot juice can increase your body's production of glutathione, which is a powerful antioxidant that supports detoxification in the body.

1 beetroot, washed and stem removed

5 medium carrots

1 small cucumber

1 lemon

1 inch of fresh ginger root, peeled

1 inch of fresh turmeric root, peeled

1 apple or pear (optional)

IMMUNE-BOOSTING JUICE

Carrot juice is particularly beneficial for eye health. It's a good source of beta-carotene and lutein, which have been shown to protect the surface of the eye, contribute to strong vision, and reduce the risk of eye disorders.[2]

6 carrots

2 large oranges, peeled

1 inch of fresh ginger root, peeled

1 inch of fresh turmeric root, peeled

GREEN CABBAGE JUICE

Raw green cabbage contains isocyanates, which are a group of compounds that support the liver to detoxify and accelerate the elimination of toxins from the body.

¼ head green cabbage

½ head romaine lettuce leaves

3 carrots

1 apple, stem and core removed

1 inch of fresh ginger root, peeled

BEETROOT ENERGIZER

Again, beetroot is the star ingredient in this juice. Not only does it help detoxify your liver, but it has also been shown to increase stamina in exercise.[1] This is because of a compound called nitrate that helps to relax blood vessels, increase blood flow, and promote oxygen uptake by muscles.

2 beetroots, washed and stems removed

2 large oranges, peeled

1 inch of fresh ginger root, peeled

1 inch of fresh turmeric root, peeled

GROUNDING EVENING JUICE

Parsley is an everyday herb with a lot of health benefits. In animal studies, it has been shown to enhance liver function and boost antioxidant levels.[3] It's also a very rich source of vitamin C. In fact, 100 grams of parsley contains 133 milligrams of vitamin C compared to oranges, which contain 53 milligrams of vitamin C per 100 grams.

¼ bunch celery

½ head romaine lettuce leaves

1 carrot

1 small beetroot, washed and stem removed

½ bunch parsley

REST EASY JUICE

Bell peppers are the secret ingredient in this juice. They are rich in antioxidants, especially vitamin C and carotenoids, which provide a number of health benefits, such as improved eye health and reduced risk of several chronic diseases.

1 head romaine lettuce

3 small carrots

1 small beetroot, washed and stem removed

1 red bell pepper, cored

1 lemon, peeled

1 inch of fresh ginger root, peeled

SMOOTHIES

FOOD MATTERS SIGNATURE GREEN SMOOTHIE

Want to start your day feeling invigorated and full of energy? The Food Matters Green Smoothie is the perfect breakfast for that refreshed, ready-to-take-on-the-day feeling!

SERVES: **1**	YIELD: **2 CUPS**	PREP TIME: **5 MINUTES**	COOK TIME: **NONE**

1 medium banana, peeled and sliced, preferably frozen

½ avocado

1 cup baby spinach

1 tablespoon hemp seeds

1 tablespoon nut butter

1 Medjool date, pitted

1½ cups unsweetened plant-based milk of choice (coconut, almond, oat)

1 pinch unrefined sea salt

OPTIONAL TOPPINGS

½ teaspoon ground cinnamon

¼ teaspoon ground ginger

¼ teaspoon ground nutmeg

1. Blend together all the ingredients until smooth.

2. If the consistency of the smoothie is too thick, slowly add more plant-based milk to the blender.

3. To add an extra boost to your smoothie, pick 1 or 2 of the optional spices.

FM TIP: Avocado is a little powerhouse that's discreet in flavor. It is rich in essential fatty acids that are integral for cell and hormone function, and it will keep you fuller for longer.

BERRY-RICH SMOOTHIE

Created to keep the cravings at bay, this delicious smoothie is packed with the nutrients you need to keep going through to your next meal.

SERVES: **1**　　　　YIELD: **2 CUPS**　　　　PREP TIME: **5 MINUTES**　　　　COOK TIME: **NONE**

---

1 medium banana, peeled and sliced, preferably frozen

1 cup frozen mixed berries

1 cup baby spinach

1 tablespoon hemp seeds

1 tablespoon nut butter

1½ cups unsweetened plant based milk of choice (coconut, almond, oat)

OPTIONAL TOPPINGS

2 tablespoons coconut yogurt

2 tablespoons Homemade Granola (page 216)

1. Blend together all the ingredients until smooth.

2. Drink as is or serve in a bowl topped with a swirl of coconut yogurt and Homemade Granola.

FM TIP: Berries are rich in antioxidants, which help your body fight cell damage, premature aging, and oxidative stress.[4]

CHOCOLATE LOVERS SMOOTHIE BOWL

Chocolate lovers rejoice! This smoothie bowl is packed with goodness but will have you feeling like you are enjoying an indulgent treat.

SERVES: **1**   YIELD: **2 CUPS**   PREP TIME: **5 MINUTES**   COOK TIME: **NONE**

---

1 medium banana, peeled, sliced, and frozen

¼ avocado

1 tablespoon unsweetened cocoa powder

1 tablespoon hemp seeds

1 cup unsweetened plant-based milk of choice (coconut, almond, oat)

1 pinch unrefined sea salt

1 teaspoon chia seeds

OPTIONAL TOPPINGS

2 tablespoons Homemade Granola (page 216)

2 tablespoons coconut yogurt

1 tablespoon frozen mixed berries

1 tablespoon hemp seeds

2 squares dark chocolate

1. Blend together all the ingredients until smooth.

2. If the smoothie is a little thick, add more plant-based milk to the blender to achieve your desired consistency.

3. Pour into a bowl, top with Homemade Granola, a dollop of coconut yogurt, mixed berries, and a sprinkle of hemp seeds.

FM TIP: Raw cacao has powerful anti-inflammatory properties, as it is rich in antioxidants and other vital compounds.

BERRY SMOOTHIE BOWL

A filling breakfast smoothie bowl topped with our favorite Homemade Granola.

SERVES: **1**   YIELD: **2 CUPS**   PREP TIME: **5 MINUTES**   COOK TIME: **NONE**

---

1 medium banana, peeled, sliced, and frozen

1 cup frozen mixed berries

1 cup baby spinach

1 tablespoon nut butter

1 tablespoon hemp seeds

1 cup unsweetened plant-based milk of choice (coconut, almond, oat)

2 tablespoons coconut yogurt

OPTIONAL TOPPINGS

½ cup fresh or frozen strawberries, halved and tops removed

¼ cup Homemade Granola (page 216)

½ banana, sliced

½ tablespoon hemp seeds

1. Blend together all the ingredients until smooth.

2. If the smoothie consistency is too thick, add a little more plant-based milk to the blender until your preferred consistency is achieved.

3. Top with the strawberries, Homemade Granola, banana, and hemp seeds.

FM TIP. Boost any breakfast smoothie with a dose of hemp seeds for extra protein, omega-3 fatty acids, and fiber.

MAGNESIUM BOOSTING SMOOTHIE

A great smoothie with healthy fats, protein, and magnesium to drink post-workout to help you recharge your energy stores and assist with muscle recovery.

SERVES: **1**   YIELD: **2 CUPS**   PREP TIME: **5 MINUTES**   COOK TIME: **NONE**

1 medium banana, peeled, sliced, and frozen

1 tablespoon raw cacao powder

1 tablespoon pepitas

1 tablespoon tahini

1 teaspoon ground cinnamon

1 cup unsweetened plant-based milk of choice (coconut, almond, oat)

½ cup baby spinach

1 tablespoon plant-based protein powder (optional)

Blend all the ingredients together and drink immediately.

FM TIP: Raw cacao powder is one of the highest plant-based sources of magnesium and is amazing for energy, muscle recovery, and heart health.

HEMP & VANILLA BREAKFAST SMOOTHIE

Tiny little hemp seeds in this breakfast smoothie contain vitamins, minerals, and polyunsaturated fatty acids and are a great vegetarian source of protein and omega-3.

SERVES: **1**	YIELD: **2 CUPS**	PREP TIME: **5 MINUTES**	COOK TIME: **NONE**

¼ cup frozen cauliflower

1 Medjool date, pitted

½ cup unsweetened plant-based milk of choice (coconut, almond, oat)

1 cup filtered cold water

2 tablespoons hemp protein

2 tablespoons oats

1 teaspoon vanilla extract

½ teaspoon ground cinnamon

Blend all the ingredients together until smooth and creamy.

FM TIP: Frozen cauliflower in smoothies is a good way to boost your vegetable intake!

PINEAPPLE & TURMERIC ANTI-INFLAMMATORY SMOOTHIE

So you've read about the health benefits of turmeric, but you're not sure how you can use it? Here's a smoothie recipe that uses it in the most refreshing way while offering a host of health benefits!

| SERVES: **1** | YIELD: **2 CUPS** | PREP TIME: **5 MINUTES** | COOK TIME: **NONE** |

1 cup diced pineapple

1 teaspoon turmeric, powder or freshly grated

1 tablespoon chia seeds

1 tablespoon shredded coconut

½ lime, peeled

1 cup water or coconut water

1 teaspoon maca powder

1 pinch black pepper

Blend all the ingredients together until smooth and creamy.

FM TIP: Using black pepper along with turmeric is essential for helping with the absorption of curcumin, which is the compound responsible for turmeric's health benefits. Turmeric helps detox the body, lower inflammation, and support a healthy immune system. Pineapples offer some surprising benefits because they contain the natural enzyme bromelain, which supports the digestive system in breaking down and absorbing nutrients from the food we eat.

GREEN GODDESS BOWL

How do we keep our skin glowing and gorgeous, naturally? Our favorite way to feed our skin and keep it looking fresh is through the food we eat. Our Green Goddess Bowl is packed with anti-inflammatory ingredients to get that glow.

SERVES: **1**   YIELD: **2 CUPS**   PREP TIME: **5 MINUTES**   COOK TIME: **NONE**

1 medium banana, peeled, sliced, and frozen

1 small frozen zucchini

1 small avocado, pitted

1 large handful baby spinach

1 to 2 teaspoons superfood greens powder

1 cup unsweetened plant-based milk of choice (coconut, almond, oat)

1 handful mint leaves

1 to 2 cups ice

1. Blend all the ingredients together until smooth and creamy.

2. Serve in a bowl and top with your favorite toppings, such as our Homemade Granola, hemp seeds, berries, or sliced banana.

FM TIP: Adding an extra boost of a superfood greens powder to your smoothie is a great way to get more nutrients and minerals into your diet! Want to learn more? Read our superfood greens buying guide on FoodMatters.com.

PLANT-BASED MILKS

Making your own plant-based milk may seem a little daunting, but we're here to show you how easy it is to do and how delicious they are! Store-bought versions of plant-based milk are often filled with extra sugar, preservatives, and additives. These ingredients may be present in small quantities, but they often impair the gut barrier, causing digestive problems.

PLANT-BASED MILK

These plant-based milk recipes are some of our favorites. All these nuts and seeds offer an array of health benefits.

1. Soak seeds or nuts for 7 to 12 hours. (See "The Benefits of Soaking and Activating Nuts and Seeds," page 54.)

2. Drain and rinse soaked seeds or nuts.

3. Blend all the ingredients together in a blender or juicer for 30 seconds to 1 minute until the milk is smooth and creamy.

4. OPTIONAL: Strain through a nut milk bag, or pour straight into glass bottles for storage in the fridge if you don't mind pulp in your milk.

PUMPKIN SEED MILK

1 cup pumpkin seeds
(soaked overnight)

6 cups filtered water

3 pitted Medjool
dates or 1
tablespoon raw
honey

1 teaspoon vanilla
extract

½ teaspoon sea salt

> **FM TIP:** Pumpkin seeds are high in
> minerals such as magnesium, phosphorus,
> manganese, zinc, iron, and copper, as
> well as in essential fatty acids.[5]

HEMP SEED MILK

½ cup hulled
hemp seeds

4 cups filtered
water

1 pinch sea salt

1 Medjool date,
pitted

½ teaspoon vanilla
extract (optional)

> **FM TIP:** Rich in essential fatty acids and
> known for improving heart health and
> reducing cholesterol, hemp seeds are
> also rich in protein and fiber.[7]

BRAZIL NUT MILK

1 cup Brazil nuts
(soaked overnight)

4 cups filtered water

2 Medjool dates,
pitted

1 teaspoon vanilla
extract

½ teaspoon sea salt

½ tablespoon
coconut oil

> **FM TIP:** Brazil nuts are one of the
> richest sources of selenium in the food
> world, making them a great addition to
> your diet to help boost your immune
> system. They also contain a complete
> amino acid profile, making them a
> great plant-based protein source.[6]

CASHEW MILK

1 cup cashews
(soaked overnight)

4 cups filtered water

2 Medjool dates,
pitted

1 teaspoon vanilla
extract

1 pinch sea salt

> **FM TIP:** Cashews offer many vitamins
> and minerals including zinc,
> phosphorus, iron, manganese, and
> copper and are particularly rich
> in vitamin E, making them a great
> addition to your diet to protect and
> nourish your skin from the inside out.[8]

BREAKFAST

GREEN BREAKFAST BOWL WITH AVOCADO

Broccoli for breakfast? Sounds odd, but trust us, this Green Breakfast Bowl with Avocado will leave you feeling full and energized to start the day! Adding extra greens at breakfast is an easy way to get ahead with your veg intake for the day.

| SERVES: 1 | YIELD: **2 CUPS** | PREP TIME: **5 MINUTES** | COOK TIME: **10 MINUTES** |

2 teaspoons extra virgin olive oil, divided

¼ head broccoli, finely chopped

½ cup baby spinach, roughly chopped

½ lemon

½ cup quinoa, cooked

¼ bunch mint leaves, de-stemmed and finely chopped

¼ bunch parsley leaves, de-stemmed and finely chopped

1 organic free-range egg

½ avocado, sliced

1 teaspoon hemp seeds

1 teaspoon sesame seeds

1 tablespoon sauerkraut

1 pinch unrefined sea salt and black pepper, to taste

1. Heat 1 teaspoon olive oil in a medium frying pan on high heat. Add the broccoli, spinach, and a squeeze of fresh lemon juice. Then add the quinoa and stir for a couple of minutes until the greens are cooked but still vibrant in color. Mix in the mint and parsley and pour into your bowl.

2. Return the frying pan to the stove. Heat 1 teaspoon olive oil and crack the egg into the pan. Let the egg cook until the edges are crispy, then place a lid on the frying pan and allow the egg to continue to steam to your liking. This will be about 2 minutes for a runny yolk or up to 3 minutes for a medium yolk.

3. Top the greens with the fried egg and avocado. Add the hemp seeds, sesame seeds, sauerkraut, salt, and pepper, to taste.

GLUTEN-FREE VEGAN PANCAKES WITH SEASONAL FRUIT & COCONUT YOGURT

Vegan pancakes are tricky to nail, but this recipe is so simple that it has become a favorite with the Food Matters team.

SERVES: **2**	YIELD: **8 PANCAKES**	PREP TIME: **5 MINUTES**	COOK TIME: **10 MINUTES**

½ cup cassava flour

½ teaspoon baking soda

1 pinch unrefined sea salt

½ cup unsweetened plant-based milk of choice (coconut, almond, oat)

1 tablespoon pure maple syrup

1 tablespoon coconut oil

1 cup fresh berries or seasonal fruit

2 to 3 tablespoons coconut yogurt (optional)

1. Combine the cassava flour, baking soda, and salt in a large bowl.

2. Pour in the milk and maple syrup, whisking together, and gradually pour in ¼ cup water.

3. Heat a large frying pan over medium-high heat, grease with the coconut oil, and drop ¼ cup of the pancake mixture into the pan.

4. Cook until bubbles form, flip, and cook for another minute. Repeat until all the mixture is used up.

5. Add the berries to the same frying pan and add ¼ cup water. Cook down the berries over medium heat until a berry sauce forms.

6. Serve the pancakes topped with the berry sauce and coconut yogurt.

FM TIP: Cassava flour, also known as manioc flour, is readily available in health food stores. It's the perfect gluten substitute, as it has a very similar texture to wheat flour.

COCONUT BLUEBERRY CHIA PUDDING WITH GRANOLA

Prep this breakfast the night before for an easy, on-the-go option when you're in a rush!

SERVES: **2**	YIELD: **2 CUPS**	PREP TIME: **OVERNIGHT**	COOK TIME: **10 MINUTES**

2 cups fresh or frozen blueberries, thawed

1 ½ cups unsweetened plant-based milk of choice (coconut, almond, oat)

1 tablespoon pure maple syrup

¼ teaspoon ground cardamom

¼ teaspoon ground nutmeg

¼ teaspoon ground cinnamon

1 pinch unrefined sea salt

¼ cup chia seeds

¼ cup Homemade Granola (page 216)

1. Add the blueberries to a medium mixing bowl along with the plant-based milk, maple syrup, cardamom, nutmeg, cinnamon, and salt. Using a metal fork, mash ingredients together.

2. Pour the mixture into 2 large sealable jars or containers.

3. Add the chia seeds, shake, then refrigerate overnight.

4. Serve with Homemade Granola.

FM TIP: Chia pudding is one of the simplest, healthiest breakfast options to make ahead of time. Get creative and add your fave fruit in the morning! Chia seeds are a great source of plant-based protein, amazing for the digestive system, and rich in omega-3s.

FOOD MATTERS
2-INGREDIENT PANCAKES

Quick, easy, and delicious! All it takes is two ingredients, banana and egg, to create the foundation for an amazing breakfast loaded with protein. A filling, everyday treat!

SERVES: **1**	YIELD: **4 PANCAKES**	PREP TIME: **2 MINUTES**	COOK TIME: **5 MINUTES**

2 organic free-range eggs

1 banana, peeled, chopped roughly

1 tablespoon coconut oil

½ cup fresh or frozen mixed berries

1 tablespoon coconut yogurt

1 tablespoon nut butter

1 tablespoon hemp seeds

1. Whisk the eggs in a bowl. Add the banana and mash together to form a batter.

2. Heat 1 tablespoon coconut oil in a frying pan and pour in 2 to 3 tablespoons of the batter to create a thin pancake. Let the pancake cook for 1 to 2 minutes or until bubbles form, then flip and cook for another 1 to 2 minutes. Repeat until all the batter is gone.

3. In the same frying pan, add the mixed berries with ¼ cup water and stir and mash until a jam-like consistency is achieved.

4. Serve the pancakes topped with the berries, a dollop of coconut yogurt, nut butter, and hemp seeds.

FM TIP: Slightly underripe bananas work best for this recipe, as the starch content acts as a binding agent for the mixture.

JAMES'S BREKKIE WRAP

This breakfast wrap is one of James's favorites for a quick and healthy breakfast. If you haven't tried our Homemade Gluten-Free Wraps (page 220), then we encourage you to whip them up for this recipe!

SERVES: **1**   YIELD: **1 WRAP**   PREP TIME: **2 MINUTES**   COOK TIME: **5 MINUTES**

2 organic free-range eggs

1 pinch unrefined sea salt and black pepper

1 cup baby spinach leaves

1 ½ teaspoons extra virgin olive oil

1 gluten-free wrap (page 220 or store-bought)

¼ avocado

1 tablespoon sauerkraut

1 tablespoon paleo mayonnaise

1. In a large bowl, whisk the eggs and add a pinch of salt and pepper to season. Then add the baby spinach leaves.

2. Heat the oil in a frying pan set over medium heat. Pour in the egg mixture and continually fold the eggs from the outer edge for 2 to 3 minutes or until cooked through.

3. On the wrap, spread the avocado in the center, lay the cooked eggs on top, and add your preferred amount of sauerkraut and paleo mayonnaise.

4. Fold up the bottom of the wrap, pull in the sides, and enjoy!

EASY ZUCCHINI FRITTERS

There is something so perfect about a fritter. Something so small can be the best little flavor bomb and a filling breakfast option—plus, leftovers make a great snack!

SERVES: **2**	YIELD: **8 FRITTERS**	PREP TIME: **10 MINUTES**	COOK TIME: **5 MINUTES**

2 pinches unrefined sea salt, divided

2 medium zucchini, grated

½ yellow onion, finely diced

1 tablespoon almond meal

2 organic free-range eggs

1 pinch black pepper

1 tablespoon extra virgin olive oil, plus additional to taste

2 cups baby spinach leaves

½ lemon

1 tablespoon sauerkraut (optional)

1. Add a pinch of salt to the zucchini and allow to sit for 10 minutes to draw out extra water.

2. Using your hands, squeeze the zucchini to remove excess water, discarding the liquid. Add the onion, almond meal, eggs, and a pinch of salt and pepper until you have a thick, pancake-like batter.

3. Heat 1 tablespoon oil in a frying pan over medium heat. Pour the fritter mixture into the frying pan in 8 even scoops. Cook for 5 minutes on each side, or until golden.

4. Divide the fritters in half and serve with 1 cup baby spinach leaves, a squeeze of lemon, a drizzle of oil, and sauerkraut.

POACHED PEAR
WITH SPICED ROASTED NUTS

A breakfast that tastes more like a dessert? Yes, please! Poached pears feel like such a treat. We've ditched the refined sugar and replaced it with a small amount of pure maple syrup that gives the pears a rich, caramelized flavor.

SERVES: **1**	YIELD: **1 PEAR**	PREP TIME: **10 MINUTES**	COOK TIME: **10 MINUTES**

1 teaspoon ground cinnamon

1 teaspoon ground ginger

1 tablespoon pure maple syrup

1 teaspoon lemon rind (optional)

Juice of ½ lemon

1 pear, halved

½ cup coconut yogurt

¼ cup Spiced Roasted Nuts (page 113)

1. Combine ½ cup water, cinnamon, ginger, maple syrup, lemon rind, lemon juice, and pear in a saucepan. Bring to a boil. Reduce to a simmer, cover, and cook the pear for 5 minutes.

2. Serve the poached pear with coconut yogurt and Spiced Roasted Nuts.

MEAL PREP HACK: Make a batch of Poached Pears with Spiced Roasted Nuts at the start of the week, and you'll have a very quick and tasty breakfast for those mornings you're in a rush!

SPICED ROASTED NUTS

This is one recipe that will become a regular in your recipe bank! You don't have to use this just for breakfast recipes either; these spiced nuts are great to have on hand as a healthy snack.

SERVES: **4**   YIELD: **2 CUPS**   PREP TIME: **2 MINUTES**   COOK TIME: **15 MINUTES**

½ **cup activated almonds, chopped**

½ **cup activated walnuts, chopped**

½ **cup activated Brazil nuts, chopped**

1 teaspoon coconut oil, melted if solidified

½ **teaspoon ground cinnamon**

½ **teaspoon ground ginger**

1 pinch unrefined sea salt

1 tablespoon pure maple syrup

1. Preheat the oven to 350°F (180°C) and line a large baking sheet with parchment paper.

2. Combine all the ingredients in a bowl. Scatter evenly on the lined baking sheet and bake for 10 to 12 minutes or until golden brown.

3. Remove from the oven and set aside to cool for 15 minutes.

4. Store in an airtight container or jar in a cool, dry place for up to 2 weeks.

BLUEBERRY CHIA BOWL WITH CARAMELIZED SESAME BANANAS

Full of fiber, healthy fats, and gluten free, its luxurious flavor makes this treat taste a little bit naughty.

SERVES: **1**	YIELD: **2 CUPS**	PREP TIME: **5 MINUTES**	COOK TIME: **8 MINUTES**

CHIA BOWL

½ cup blueberries, fresh or thawed if frozen

1 cup unsweetened plant-based milk of choice (coconut, almond, oat)

3 tablespoons chia seeds

1 teaspoon ground cardamom

1 teaspoon ground nutmeg

1 pinch unrefined sea salt

2 tablespoons coconut yogurt

1 tablespoon nut butter

CARAMELIZED BANANA

½ tablespoon coconut oil

1 tablespoon pure maple syrup

1 tablespoon activated almonds, chopped

1 tablespoon sesame seeds

1 tablespoon activated walnuts, chopped

1 banana, peeled, sliced in half lengthwise

1. In a large bowl, mash the blueberries with a fork, then add the plant-based milk, chia seeds, cardamom, nutmeg, and salt. Stir to combine and let sit for 20 minutes.

2. To make the caramelized bananas, heat the coconut oil and maple syrup in a frying pan. Add the almonds, sesame seeds, and walnuts, stirring until they start to become sticky.

3. Make room in the center of the nut mixture and add the banana halves. Heat for just a minute on each side or until the bananas begin to caramelize. Remove the pan from the heat.

4. Add the prepared blueberry chia to a bowl, top with the coconut yogurt, and place the caramelized bananas in the middle.

5. Drizzle the sticky nut mixture over the bananas, then top with nut butter.

KICKSTARTER GREEN CHILI SCRAMBLE

If you need a kick start to your morning, then this one is for you! Packed with protein, fiber, and a hit of chili, you will be left feeling satiated long after your meal is done.

SERVES: **1**	YIELD: **1 CUP**	PREP TIME: **5 MINUTES**	COOK TIME: **5 MINUTES**

2 organic free-range eggs

1 pinch unrefined sea salt and black pepper

½ long red chili, finely chopped

¼ bunch parsley leaves, chopped

½ tablespoon extra virgin olive oil

¼ cup frozen peas, thawed

½ medium zucchini, diced

1 cup baby spinach leaves

¼ lemon

½ tablespoon hemp seeds (optional)

1 tablespoon sauerkraut (optional)

1. Whisk the eggs, salt, pepper, chili, and parsley in a medium bowl.

2. Warm the oil in a medium pan using medium to high heat.

3. Add the peas and zucchini to the pan and stir for 5 minutes.

4. Pour the egg mixture into the pan, and, using a spatula, gently move the mixture around to keep it from firming up at the base and sides.

5. When the eggs are only two thirds cooked and still runny (about 2 to 3 minutes), remove them from heat.

6. Leave them to continue to "cook" in their own heat for another minute or two.

7. Serve with the baby spinach leaves, a squeeze of lemon juice, hemp seeds, and sauerkraut.

FM TIP: Organic free-range eggs are a rich source of full-spectrum protein, healthy fats, and micronutrients such as iron and B$_{12}$. You can also switch out the eggs for a softened tofu to make a delicious vegan version.

CREAMY CINNAMON & APPLE OATMEAL

Oatmeal has always been a breakfast staple in our house. This recipe is rich, creamy, and topped with caramelized cinnamon apples.

SERVES: **1**	YIELD: **1 CUP**	PREP TIME: **5 MINUTES**	COOK TIME: **10 MINUTES**

1 teaspoon coconut oil

1 tablespoon pure maple syrup

1 apple, cored and diced

½ teaspoon ground cinnamon, divided

½ cup unsweetened plant-based milk of choice (coconut, almond, oat)

½ cup gluten-free instant oats

1 pinch unrefined sea salt

¼ cup Spiced Roasted Nuts (page 113)

1. Heat the coconut oil in a small pan and combine the maple syrup, apples, and ¼ teaspoon cinnamon. Bring to a simmer over medium-low heat, continuously stirring for 7 to 8 minutes or until the apples are caramelized. Remove from the heat and place the caramelized apples in a bowl.

2. Add the plant-based milk, oats, ½ cup water, and salt to the same saucepan over medium-low heat. Cook until creamy, stirring continuously.

3. Serve the creamy oats topped with the caramelized apples and Spiced Roasted Nuts.

FM TIP: If oats aren't for you, swap these out for buckwheat.

MUSHROOM, KALE & QUINOA BREKKIE BOWL WITH CASHEW HEMP BASIL PESTO

Loaded with greens, wholesome quinoa, and gorgeous mushrooms, topped with our go-to Cashew Hemp Pesto, this breakfast bowl is the king of breakfast bowls.

SERVES: 1	YIELD: 1 ½ CUPS	PREP TIME: 5 MINUTES	COOK TIME: 10 MINUTES

2 teaspoons extra virgin olive oil, divided

2 kale leaves, destemmed and roughly chopped

1 cup baby spinach

½ cup mixed mushrooms (shiitake, Swiss brown, enoki)

2 teaspoons extra virgin olive oil, divided

¼ cup quinoa, cooked

Unrefined sea salt and black pepper, to taste

½ lemon

1 organic free-range egg

1 teaspoon sesame seeds

1 teaspoon hemp seeds

1 tablespoon Cashew Hemp Basil Pesto (page 208)

1 tablespoon paleo mayonnaise (optional)

1 tablespoon sauerkraut (optional)

1. Heat 1 teaspoon oil in a medium frying pan on high heat. Add the kale, spinach, and mushrooms and sauté for 5 to 10 minutes. Add the cooked quinoa to the frying pan and stir until warmed. Remove from the heat and transfer the mixture to a separate dish. Season with salt and pepper and a squeeze of lemon juice.

2. Return the frying pan to the stove. Add 1 teaspoon oil and, once the pan is heated, crack the egg into the pan. Let the egg cook until the edges are crispy, then place a lid on the frying pan and allow the egg to continue to steam to your liking. This will be about 2 minutes for a runny yolk and up to 3 minutes for a medium yolk.

3. Top the greens and mushrooms with the fried egg. Add the sesame seeds, hemp seeds, Cashew Hemp Basil Pesto, paleo mayonnaise, and sauerkraut.

FM TIP: Mushrooms are a powerhouse of nutrients, especially when grown in optimized conditions. The soil and environment where mushrooms grow provide essential minerals and potent healing properties. You can also boost the vitamin D content of your mushrooms by sunning them in direct sunlight for 20 minutes before storing them.

SPINACH & HARISSA SHAKSHUKA

Inspired by our travels, our spin on shakshuka celebrates the flavors of the Middle East and North Africa.

SERVES: **2**	YIELD: **3 CUPS**	PREP TIME: **10 MINUTES**	COOK TIME: **30 MINUTES**

2 tablespoons extra virgin olive oil

1 small yellow onion, thinly sliced

1 red bell pepper, seeded and diced

Unrefined sea salt and black pepper, to taste

3 medium garlic cloves, minced

½ teaspoon smoked paprika

½ teaspoon ground cumin

One 14-ounce (400 grams) can crushed tomatoes, with liquid

2 tablespoons harissa paste

1 cup baby spinach, chopped

4 organic free-range eggs

¼ bunch parsley, destemmed and roughly chopped

¼ cup cherry tomatoes, halved

½ avocado, sliced

1. Preheat the oven to 355°F (180°C).

2. Heat the oil over medium heat in a medium oven-safe frying pan. Add the onion, red pepper, salt, and pepper. Cook for 4 to 5 minutes or until the onion is soft and translucent.

3. Reduce the heat to medium-low and add the garlic, paprika, cumin, tomatoes, and harissa paste. Simmer for 10 minutes or until the sauce begins to thicken.

4. Add the spinach and stir through. Make 4 holes in the sauce and gently crack an egg in each hole. Bake for 20 to 25 minutes or until the eggs are cooked to your liking. If you aren't using an oven-safe frying pan, you will need to transfer the sauce mixture to an oven-safe dish and follow the step for the eggs.

5. Remove the pan from the oven and season with salt and pepper to taste.

6. Serve sprinkled with parsley and topped with cherry tomatoes and avocado.

LAURENTINE'S ISLAND BREAKFAST BOWL

Since moving to Vanuatu, Laurentine has loved experimenting with the local produce from the markets. This recipe may be a simple one, but the flavors pack a punch!

SERVES: **2**	YIELD: **1 CUP**	PREP TIME: **10 MINUTES**	COOK TIME: **NONE**

½ pineapple, peeled, cored, and diced

1 Lebanese or Persian cucumber, peeled (if nonorganic) and diced

¼ cup mint leaves, finely chopped

1 pinch unrefined sea salt

¼ teaspoon chili powder

Juice of 1 lime

Mix the pineapple, cucumber, mint, salt, and chili powder in a bowl and serve with a squeeze of fresh lime juice on top.

FM TIP: Pineapples provide a host of vitamins and minerals, including vitamins A and C, calcium, potassium, magnesium, and manganese. They also contain bromelain, which helps regulate the pancreatic secretions that aid in digestion.

BREAKFAST TACOS WITH HOMEMADE GLUTEN-FREE WRAPS

We are here to tell you that tacos do not have to be just for dinner! The breakfast taco has everything you need in a balanced breakfast: protein, fiber, healthy fats, and a nice dose of carbohydrates to fuel your body for the day.

SERVES: 2	YIELD: 4 TACOS	PREP TIME: 10 MINUTES	COOK TIME: 15 MINUTES

1 tablespoon extra virgin olive oil

2 scallions, chopped thinly

½ cup cherry tomatoes, halved

4 organic free-range eggs, beaten

1 pinch unrefined sea salt and black pepper, to taste

4 Homemade Gluten-Free Wraps (page 220)

½ avocado, sliced

2 tablespoons Salsa Verde (page 211)

1. Heat the oil in a small frying pan over medium heat.

2. Add the scallions and tomatoes, and sauté for 2 to 3 minutes or until slightly softened. Add the eggs with a pinch of sea salt and pepper, and let them cook undisturbed for a few seconds, then mix together. Continue to cook for another 2 to 3 minutes or until the eggs are cooked through.

3. While the eggs cook, lightly warm the gluten-free wraps in a medium frying pan over low-medium heat.

4. Assemble the tacos with a scoop of the egg scramble on each warmed gluten-free wrap, topped with sliced avocado and a drizzle of Salsa Verde.

FM TIP: The great thing about breakfast tacos is you can create them with anything. We love using up any roast vegetables on breakfast tacos. Fry them up with some extra spices instead of eggs for another type of nourishing meal!

FOOD MATTERS
BREAKFAST BREAD (4 WAYS)

Transitioning to gluten-free principles doesn't mean you need to cut out bread. Our Food Matters Breakfast Bread is one of the most popular recipes on our website. It's versatile, freezes well, and is gluten free, and it is packed with nourishing fats, protein, and fiber. Top it with our favorite Toast Toppers for the perfect start to your day.

SERVES: 4　　　　**YIELD: 8 TO 10 SLICES**　　　　**PREP TIME: 10 MINUTES**　　　　**COOK TIME: 40 MINUTES**

---

2 cups almond meal

⅔ cup tapioca starch or arrowroot flour

2 tablespoons flax meal

1 tablespoon chia seeds

1 teaspoon baking powder

1 pinch unrefined sea salt

3 organic free-range eggs

¼ cup coconut milk

1 tablespoon pure maple syrup

¼ cup coconut oil

1 teaspoon apple cider vinegar

1. Preheat the oven to 350° F (180° C) and line a loaf tin with parchment paper.

2. Combine the almond meal, tapioca starch, flax meal, chia seeds, baking powder, and salt in one bowl. Whisk together the eggs, milk, maple syrup, coconut oil, and apple cider vinegar in another bowl.

3. Combine the wet and dry ingredients and pour into the loaf tin.

4. Bake for 30 to 40 minutes or until golden brown on top and cooked through. Place a skewer in the center of the bread, and when the skewer comes out clean, the bread is ready.

MEAL PREP HACK: The Food Matters Breakfast Bread freezes well. It makes a great snack or breakfast that can be kept on hand in the freezer.

TOAST TOPPERS

MINT PEA HUMMUS

SERVES: **4**   YIELD: **2 CUPS**   PREPARATION TIME: **5 MINUTES**

2 cups frozen green peas, defrosted

¼ bunch fresh mint leaves

Juice of 1 lemon

1 garlic clove, crushed

2 tablespoons extra virgin olive oil

1 tablespoon tahini

1 pinch unrefined sea salt and black pepper, or to taste

1. Blanch the peas in boiling water for 1 minute or until tender, drain, and transfer to a food processor.

2. Add the mint, lemon juice, garlic, oil, and tahini to the food processor and pulse until mixed well. Season with salt and pepper.

3. Serve as a topping on your homemade Food Matters Breakfast Bread.

BREAKFAST BRUSCHETTA

SERVES: **4**   YIELD: **1 ½ CUPS**   PREPARATION TIME: **5 MINUTES**

1 avocado, peeled and pitted

2 pinches unrefined sea salt and black pepper, divided

1 cup cherry tomatoes, halved

½ bunch fresh basil leaves, roughly chopped

1 tablespoon balsamic vinegar

1 tablespoon extra virgin olive oil

1. Smash the avocado in a small bowl, then add a pinch of salt and pepper.

2. In another small bowl, mix the tomatoes, basil leaves, balsamic vinegar, oil, and a pinch of salt and pepper.

3. To serve, spread a layer of the smashed avocado on your homemade Food Matters Breakfast Bread, then top with the tomato bruschetta mix.

SAUTÉED MUSHROOMS

SERVES: **4**   YIELD: **1 CUP**   PREPARATION TIME: **5 MINUTES**

2 tablespoon extra virgin olive oil, divided

1 cup mixed mushrooms, thinly sliced

1 teaspoon dried thyme

1 garlic clove, crushed

¼ teaspoon unrefined sea salt, or to taste

¼ teaspoon black pepper, or to taste

2 tablespoons chopped parsley

1. Heat 1 tablespoon oil in a small frying pan over medium heat.

2. Add the mushrooms, thyme, garlic, salt, and pepper, and cook, stirring for 3 to 4 minutes or until the mushroom mixture softens.

3. Spoon the mushroom mixture on your homemade Food Matters Breakfast Bread and sprinkle with fresh parsley.

HARISSA BAKED BEANS

SERVES: **4**   YIELD: **3 CUPS**   PREPARATION TIME: **10 MINUTES**

1 tablespoon extra virgin olive oil

1 garlic clove, crushed

2 tablespoons tomato paste

1 teaspoon harissa paste

1 teaspoon ground cumin

1 teaspoon smoked paprika

One 14-ounce (400 grams) can diced tomatoes, with liquid

One 14-ounce (400 grams) can cannellini beans, drained and rinsed

¼ teaspoon unrefined sea salt, or to taste

¼ teaspoon black pepper, or to taste

1. Heat the oil in a large saucepan over medium heat, then add the garlic. Sauté for a few seconds, then stir in the tomato paste, harissa paste, cumin, and paprika.

2. Add the tomatoes and cannellini beans, along with ½ cup filtered water. Season with salt and pepper, then bring to a simmer and cook, stirring occasionally, for 10 minutes or until the beans are thickened and reduced.

3. Serve on top of your homemade Food Matters Breakfast Bread.

MAINS

MARINATED TEMPEH SKEWERS WITH GREEN APPLE SLAW

If you haven't tried tempeh before, this recipe will make you fall in love with it. Marinated in tamari, ginger, and maple syrup, these Asian-flavored skewers pack a flavor punch!

SERVES: 2	YIELD: 6 SKEWERS AND 3 CUPS SLAW	PREP TIME: 15 MINUTES	COOK TIME: 15 MINUTES

2 tablespoons tamari

1 inch of fresh ginger root, grated

1 tablespoon pure maple syrup

1 garlic clove, grated

One 10-ounce (300 grams) package tempeh, cubed

¼ small head red cabbage, thinly sliced

1 green apple, thinly sliced

¼ bunch cilantro, destemmed, roughly chopped

1 scallion, finely sliced

1 tablespoon raisins

Juice of 1 lime

1 tablespoon hulled tahini

2 teaspoons apple cider vinegar

1 pinch unrefined sea salt and black pepper

1 teaspoon coconut oil

1 tablespoon activated walnuts, roughly chopped (optional)

1. Soak 6 bamboo skewers in water while you prepare the tempeh and slaw. This step will prevent the skewers from burning during the cooking process.

2. Prepare the marinade by whisking together the tamari, ginger, maple syrup, and garlic.

3. Add the tempeh to the marinade and stir to coat. Set aside to marinate for at least 10 minutes while you prepare the slaw.

4. To prepare the slaw, mix the cabbage, apple, cilantro, scallion, and raisins in a large bowl.

5. To prepare the dressing, mix the lime juice, tahini, 1 tablespoon water, and apple cider vinegar in a bowl until creamy. Add a little more water to the dressing if the consistency is too thick. Season with salt and pepper. Add to the slaw and mix through until evenly coated.

6. Thread 3 to 4 cubes of the marinated tempeh onto each skewer.

7. Heat the coconut oil in a frying pan over medium heat. After 1 minute, arrange the skewers in the frying pan and cook until brown on each side, about 3 to 5 minutes.

8. Serve the skewers with the slaw and walnuts.

FM TIP: For the tempeh to soak up extra flavor, marinate it the night before. Store in the fridge until you're ready to fry up the tempeh.

GINGER & CASHEW VEGGIE STIR-FRY

Stir-fries are a great option when it comes to fast midweek dinners! They can be created out of nearly any vegetables you have on hand and a simple zingy sauce.

SERVES: 2	YIELD: **4 CUPS**	PREP TIME: **10 MINUTES**	COOK TIME: **15 MINUTES**

3 tablespoons tamari

½ inch of fresh ginger root, grated

1 tablespoon pure maple syrup

2 teaspoons sesame oil, divided

¼ long red chili, seeded and thinly sliced

½ yellow onion, thinly sliced

1 garlic clove, crushed

¼ teaspoon black pepper

1 cup green beans, trimmed

½ red bell pepper (capsicum), core removed and thinly sliced

1 small zucchini, thinly sliced

1 cup broccoli florets

½ cup brown basmati rice, uncooked

½ cup basil leaves

¼ cup raw unsalted cashews, activated

½ lime

1. Prepare the stir-fry sauce by mixing the tamari, ginger, maple syrup, and 1 teaspoon sesame oil.

2. Heat a wok or large frying pan over high heat.

3. Sauté 1 teaspoon sesame oil and the red chili, onion, garlic, and pepper for 2 minutes or until they begin to soften.

4. Add the green beans, bell pepper, zucchini, and broccoli, and stir-fry for another 4 to 5 minutes or until tender but still crispy and colorful.

5. Toss in the sauce, combining thoroughly to coat all vegetables.

6. In a medium saucepan, combine the rice with 1 cup water and bring to a boil. Stir once, cover with a tight-fitting lid, and reduce heat to low. Simmer for 20 minutes. (Do not lift the lid or stir.) Remove from the heat and let stand, covered, for 5 minutes. Fluff with a fork and serve with the stir-fried veggies, basil, and cashews, topped with a squeeze of lime.

FM TIP: Keep it light by swapping out rice for zucchini noodles. Using a simple homemade sauce such as the one here avoids the sugar, preservatives, and extra additives often packed into store-bought versions.

RICE PAPER ROLLS WITH TAMARI DIPPING SAUCE

Simple, summery rolls are a staple for any day of the week. Whether it's a shared lunch for close friends or a meal put together after a long day at work, a few vegetables and this delightful dipping sauce are all you need.

SERVES: **2**	YIELD: **12 ROLLS**	PREP TIME: **15 MINUTES**	COOK TIME: **NONE**

RICE PAPER ROLLS

1 carrot, cut into matchsticks

1 medium cucumber, deseeded, cut into matchsticks

½ red bell pepper, thinly sliced

¼ head red cabbage (1 cup), thinly sliced

½ cup snow peas, topped and tailed, cut into matchsticks

½ cup cilantro

1 avocado, thinly sliced

12 rice paper wrappers

DIPPING SAUCE

1 tablespoon tamari

Juice of ½ lime

1 tablespoon rice wine vinegar

2 teaspoons sesame seeds

1 teaspoon sesame oil

1. Set aside the carrot, cucumber, bell pepper, cabbage, snow peas, cilantro, and avocado on a plate ready for rolling. Each piece should be no longer than 3 inches.

2. In a small bowl, mix the tamari, lime juice, rice wine vinegar, sesame seeds, and sesame oil and set aside.

3. Fill a large bowl or baking dish large enough to dip your rice paper wrappers in with room temperature water.

4. Working one at a time, submerge one rice paper wrapper in the water for 10 to 30 seconds until soft and pliable.

5. Lay the wrapper on a large piece of parchment paper or on a chopping board.

6. Arrange the filling ingredients on top of each other, leaving at least an inch on the sides.

7. Bring the bottom of the wrapper up and over the pile and roll gently, making sure not to tear the delicate wrapper. Tuck the ends in as you go. Set each roll aside until all rolls have been assembled.

8. Cut the rolls in half and serve with the dipping sauce.

NAKED BURRITO BOWL

One cuisine that has stuck with us from our travels is Mexican. Although it's hard to replicate the authentic flavors and ingredients of beautiful Mexican food from the coastlines of the Yucatán Peninsula, we can still bring some of the flavors into our kitchen.

SERVES: **2**   YIELD: **4 CUPS**   PREP TIME: **10 MINUTES**   COOK TIME: **30 MINUTES**

ROASTED VEGETABLES

2 small sweet potatoes, cubed

2 tablespoons extra virgin olive oil, divided

1 teaspoon sweet smoked paprika

1 teaspoon ground cumin

½ teaspoon unrefined sea salt

1 red bell pepper, thinly sliced

1 red onion, thinly sliced

MEXI-BEAN MIX

One 14-ounce (400 grams) can black beans, drained and rinsed

Half a 14-ounce (400 grams) can garbanzo beans, drained and rinsed

1 teaspoon chili powder

1 teaspoon ground cumin

½ teaspoon unrefined sea salt

1 tablespoon extra virgin olive oil

LIME-CILANTRO QUINOA

1 cup quinoa, cooked

¼ bunch cilantro, roughly chopped

Juice of ½ lime

½ avocado

DRESSING

¼ cup hulled tahini

¼ long red chili, deseeded, thinly sliced (optional)

1 garlic clove, crushed

Juice of ½ lime

1 pinch unrefined sea salt, or to taste

(Continued)

1. Preheat the oven to 350°F (180°C).

2. Add the sweet potatoes to a bowl and toss with 1 tablespoon oil, paprika, cumin, and ½ teaspoon salt.

3. Spread the spiced sweet potatoes on a baking sheet lined with parchment paper.

4. Add the red pepper and onion to the same baking sheet, and drizzle with 1 tablespoon oil.

5. Bake for 20 to 30 minutes or until the sweet potatoes are easily pierced with a fork.

6. While the vegetables are baking, add the black beans and garbanzo beans to a medium frying pan over medium heat. Add the chili powder, cumin, salt, and a drizzle of oil, and sauté for 2 to 3 minutes to warm the beans.

7. To prepare the lime-cilantro quinoa, toss together the quinoa, cilantro, and lime juice in a bowl.

8. For each serving, assemble half the roasted veggies and half the bean mixture on top of half the lime-cilantro quinoa.

9. Whisk together all the ingredients for the dressing with 3 tablespoons warm water and drizzle on top. Top each serving with ¼ avocado and enjoy!

FM TIP: If you prefer your quinoa warm, before adding the lime and cilantro, heat a small amount of olive oil in a frying pan over medium heat and cook the quinoa for 3 to 5 minutes, or until warmed through.

BUNLESS BEETROOT BURGERS

Don't despair, you shouldn't have to miss out on a burger when you move to a more plant-based diet. This homemade alternative is a flavor bomb!

| SERVES: 2 | YIELD: **4 TO 6 PATTIES** | PREP TIME: **20 MINUTES** | COOK TIME: **15 MINUTES** |

One 14-ounce (400 grams) can brown lentils, strained

½ cup instant gluten-free oats

½ yellow onion, finely diced

½ cup activated walnuts

1 tablespoon almond meal

1 organic free-range egg

1 garlic clove, crushed

1 teaspoon sweet smoked paprika

1 teaspoon ground cumin

½ teaspoon unrefined sea salt

½ teaspoon black pepper

1 medium beetroot, grated

1 tablespoon extra virgin olive oil

2 baby romaine lettuce heads

½ avocado, sliced

1 medium cucumber, sliced into discs

1 small tomato, sliced

1 tablespoon paleo mayonnaise

1 tablespoon sauerkraut

1. Pulse the lentils, oats, onion, walnuts, almond meal, egg, garlic, paprika, cumin, salt, and pepper in a food processor or blender until combined. Transfer to a large mixing bowl. Stir the food processor contents together with the beetroot.

2. Using lightly oiled hands, form 4 to 6 small patties just under 1 inch thick.

3. Heat a frying pan over medium-high heat and add the oil to coat the bottom. Place the patties in the frying pan and cook on one side for 3 to 5 minutes. Gently flip the patties and continue to cook for another 3 to 5 minutes, or until the patties are golden brown on the outside.

4. Serve the burger patties in the lettuce leaf cups with the remaining ingredients.

FM TIP: Make and freeze burger patties ahead of time so you can pull them out for a quick, easy, and healthy midweek dinner.

GREEN PEA & MINT FRITTERS

Have you tried perfecting the fritter with no luck? It can be hard to find the right combination of texture and taste while making it all stick together in one healthy morsel, but we think this recipe is an all-round winner. The addition of peas and fresh herbs makes this perfect for an easy brunch, a weekday lunch, a midweek dinner, and everything in between.

SERVES: **2**	YIELD: **6 TO 8 FRITTERS**	PREP TIME: **10 MINUTES**	COOK TIME: **10 MINUTES**

1 cup frozen peas, thawed

¼ bunch mint, chopped

½ cup almond meal

1 scallion, sliced

2 organic free-range eggs

2 pinches unrefined sea salt and black pepper, divided

2 tablespoons extra virgin olive oil, divided

½ bunch radishes

1 medium cucumber, sliced into ribbons

2 baby romaine lettuce heads, shredded

¼ bunch mint, chopped

1 cup baby spinach

Juice of 1 lemon

½ tablespoon apple cider vinegar

1. Mix the peas, mint, almond meal, and scallion in a bowl.

2. Whisk the eggs with a pinch of salt and pepper in a separate bowl.

3. Add the eggs to the dry mixture and stir into a pancake-like batter.

4. Add 1 tablespoon oil to a frying pan set over medium to high heat. Pour 8 even scoops of the batter mixture into the pan or until batter is used. Cook the fritters for 3 to 5 minutes on each side, or until golden.

5. Create a salad with the radishes, cucumber, lettuce, mint, and spinach. Whisk together the remaining tablespoon of oil, lemon juice, apple cider vinegar, and a pinch of salt and pepper, and dress the salad.

STICKY SHIITAKE MUSHROOMS

Flavor-rich mushrooms such as shiitake are amazing for soaking up marinade flavors and creating a filling dish. Shiitake mushrooms also contain a powerful polysaccharide component that activates our immune system.

SERVING SIZE: **2**	YIELD: **3 CUPS**	PREP TIME: **15 MINUTES**	COOK TIME: **10 MINUTES**

2 cups fresh or dried shiitake mushrooms

1 bunch broccolini

½ inch of fresh ginger root, grated

2 tablespoons tamari

2 tablespoons pure maple syrup

1 tablespoon rice wine vinegar

½ teaspoon sesame seeds

1 pinch black pepper

2 tablespoons tapioca flour

1 tablespoon sesame oil

1 cup cooked quinoa

Juice of 1 lime

1. If using dried shiitake mushrooms, rehydrate them by adding the mushrooms to a bowl and covering them with boiled hot water. Make sure the mushrooms are fully immersed in the water and leave them to soak until plump, around 5 to 10 minutes. If you are using fresh shiitake mushrooms, simply slice them evenly. It looks like a lot, but mushrooms shrink significantly when cooked.

2. If you have soaked the mushrooms, dry the mushrooms as best as possible and cut into thick slices.

3. Steam the broccolini for 4 to 5 minutes.

4. In a small bowl, whisk together the ginger, tamari, maple syrup, rice wine vinegar, sesame seeds, and pepper.

5. Coat the mushrooms in the tapioca flour. Coating them well will help to crisp them slightly on the outside and create a great base for the sauce to stick to.

6. In a frying pan over medium to high heat, add the sesame oil. After 30 seconds, add the mushrooms and fry until completely crisp on both sides, about 3 to 5 minutes.

7. Pour the sauce over the mushrooms, tossing to coat well, until they become thick and sticky, about 2 to 3 more minutes. This may take a bit longer based on your mushrooms, so keep an eye on them.

8. Remove from the heat and allow to cool slightly. Toss the mushrooms with the broccolini, quinoa, and lime juice and serve.

ZUCCHINI LINGUINI WITH BASIL PESTO

Are you someone who tries and tries to be healthy but can't get enough pasta? This recipe is for you. This greened-up take on a traditional dish will hit all the right spots, so stock up on those veggies and let's get cooking.

SERVES: **2**	YIELD: **3 CUPS**	PREP TIME: **10 MINUTES**	COOK TIME: **5 MINUTES**

4 medium zucchini

1 ½ teaspoons extra virgin olive oil

2 cups baby spinach

Pinch of unrefined sea salt and black pepper

2 tablespoons Cashew Hemp Basil Pesto (page 208)

1 cup cherry tomatoes, halved

2 tablespoons hemp seeds

1. Spiralize the zucchini into noodles, or use a peeler to make ribbons.

2. Heat the oil in a large frying pan over medium heat.

3. Lightly fry the zucchini, spinach, salt, and pepper and stir until the spinach has wilted, about 1 to 2 minutes.

4. Remove from the heat, and add the Cashew Hemp Basil Pesto and tomatoes. Sprinkle with the hemp seeds before serving.

FM TIP: Optionally, you can lightly steam or blanch the zucchini noodles prior to frying.

STICKY GINGER
TEMPEH BOWL

Getting adequate protein is something that we all need to be mindful of, plant-based or not, and this delicious bowl makes it so easy! It's one for the whole family to enjoy and even goes great for lunch the next day.

SERVES: **2** | YIELD: **2 CUPS** | PREP TIME: **5 MINUTES** | COOK TIME: **25 MINUTES**

2 tablespoons tamari

1 tablespoon pure maple syrup

1 inch of fresh ginger root, grated

1 garlic clove, grated

½ long red chili, deseeded and thinly sliced

One 10-ounce (300 grams) block tempeh, sliced

1 teaspoon sesame oil

1 tablespoon extra virgin olive oil

1 pinch unrefined sea salt and black pepper

½ cup brown or white basmati rice, uncooked

1 scallion, sliced

1 lime

1. Stir the tamari, maple syrup, ginger, garlic, and chili in a saucepan over medium heat until the sauce becomes slightly sticky. Remove from the heat.

2. In a bowl, add the tempeh, drizzle with the sesame oil and half the sticky sauce, and mix to coat well. In a frying pan, fry the tempeh in olive oil and season it with salt and pepper over medium heat for 3 to 5 minutes, or until golden brown on both sides.

3. Once the tempeh has cooked, add the remaining sticky sauce to the frying pan and mix to coat well.

4. Combine the rice with 1 cup water and bring to a boil in a medium saucepan. Stir once, cover with a tight-fitting lid, and reduce the heat to low. Simmer for 20 minutes. (Do not lift the lid or stir.) Remove from the heat and let stand, covered, for 5 minutes. Fluff with a fork.

5. In a bowl, add the rice, sticky ginger tempeh, and any extra sauce, then serve with the scallion and a squeeze of lime juice.

FM TIP: We recommended choosing organic fermented tempeh or soy to receive the best health benefits for your body.

RAW PAD THAI

No cooking time for this pad thai recipe makes it an amazing option for those nights you just don't have it in you to cook! This dish is inspired by some of our favorite international flavors and our time living on a tropical island.

SERVING SIZE: **2**　　　YIELD: **3 CUPS**　　　PREP TIME: **15 MINUTES**　　　COOK TIME: **NONE**

DRESSING

⅓ cup nut butter

½ cup water

½ cup activated cashews

1 tablespoon tamari

1 tablespoon sesame oil

½ inch of fresh ginger root

1 pinch cayenne

2 tablespoons pure maple syrup

1 pinch unrefined sea salt and pepper, to taste

PAD THAI

1 medium carrot, shredded

1 cup green beans, sliced

1 cup snow peas, thinly sliced

1 medium cucumber, cut into thin strips

1 red bell pepper, cut into thin strips

½ cup fresh basil leaves

1 lime, halved

1 tablespoon pickled ginger

1 tablespoon whole, raw, activated cashews

½ tablespoon sesame seeds

1. Blend all the dressing ingredients in a food processor or blender until well combined and smooth, adding salt and pepper at the end, to taste.

2. In a bowl, combine the carrot, green beans, snow peas, cucumber, bell pepper, and basil and drizzle with the dressing. Serve with a squeeze of lime, pickled ginger, cashews, and sesame seeds.

MISO EGGPLANT & BUCKWHEAT TABBOULEH

Soul-warming, tummy-filling tabbouleh is made only from nourishing ingredients. Paired with miso-glazed eggplant, it makes the perfect dinner for the family (and is just as tasty for lunch tomorrow)!

| SERVES: **2** | YIELD: **2 CUPS** | PREP TIME: **15 MINUTES** | COOK TIME: **25 MINUTES** |

MISO EGGPLANT

2 medium eggplants

1 tablespoon apple cider vinegar

1 ½ tablespoons pure maple syrup

½ tablespoon white miso

1 inch of fresh ginger root, grated

1 teaspoon sesame oil

BUCKWHEAT TABBOULEH

½ cup buckwheat groats

1 cup broccoli, finely chopped

¼ cup parsley leaves

1 scallion, sliced

1 tablespoon sesame seeds

½ tablespoon extra virgin olive oil

Juice of ½ lemon

TAHINI CREAM

1 tablespoon hulled tahini

2 tablespoons coconut yogurt

1 pinch unrefined sea salt

1. Preheat the oven to 350°F (180°C) and line a baking sheet with parchment paper.

2. Cut the eggplants in half lengthwise and score a crosshatch pattern on the white flesh. Place on the baking sheet, white side up, and set aside.

3. In a bowl, whisk the apple cider vinegar, maple syrup, miso, ginger, and sesame oil until combined.

4. Drizzle the miso glaze over the eggplants and bake for 25 minutes.

5. While the eggplants are cooking, rinse the buckwheat under cold water, then place it in a small saucepan with 1 cup of water. Bring to a boil, then reduce to a simmer. Place a lid on the saucepan and let the buckwheat cook for 10 minutes. Drain the buckwheat.

6. Combine the buckwheat, broccoli, parsley, scallion, sesame seeds, oil, and lemon juice in a mixing bowl.

7. Prepare the tahini cream by whipping the tahini, coconut yogurt, and salt with a fork or a whisk.

8. Serve the eggplants on a bed of buckwheat tabbouleh, topped with the tahini cream.

FM TIP: Soak buckwheat overnight or for at least 4 hours in warm water 3 to 4 times the amount of buckwheat. Rinse and drain the buckwheat before use. This activation process breaks down the phytic acid that the body can have trouble digesting.

PORTOBELLO STUFFED MUSHROOMS WITH GREENS

Searching for something scrumptious, satisfying, and easy? This recipe ticks off all the boxes, hearty and packed with flavor from herbs, garlic, and crunchy cashews, and is topped with our signature Brazil Nut Parmesan.

SERVES: **2**	YIELD: **6 STUFFED MUSHROOMS**	PREP TIME: **10 MINUTES**	COOK TIME: **15 MINUTES**

6 medium portobello mushrooms

1 tablespoon extra virgin olive oil

2 garlic cloves, crushed

1 teaspoon dried thyme

1 pinch unrefined sea salt and black pepper

½ cup activated cashews

½ bunch parsley

1 bunch broccolini, trimmed

3 tablespoons Brazil Nut Parmesan (page 215)

1 tablespoon sauerkraut (optional)

1. Preheat the oven to 350°F (180°C) and line a baking sheet with parchment paper.

2. Break off the mushroom stalks, dice stems, and set aside. Clean the mushroom tops and set them on the baking sheet.

3. Sauté the oil, mushroom stalks, garlic, and thyme in a frying pan over medium heat until the mushrooms are soft and the garlic is fragrant. Season with salt and pepper. Transfer the mixture to a bowl.

4. Blitz the cashews and parsley in a food processor until they form a crumble.

5. Add the cashew crumble to the sautéed mushrooms and stir to combine.

6. Fill the mushroom tops with the cashew mushroom mix and bake for 10 minutes. After 10 minutes, place the broccolini around the stuffed mushrooms and bake for another 5 to 10 minutes.

7. Serve the portobello mushrooms with the broccolini, topped with Brazil Nut Parmesan and sauerkraut.

   FM TIP: Portobello mushrooms are packed with disease-fighting antioxidants and phytonutrients!

MOROCCAN VEGETABLE TAGINE WITH COCONUT RAITA

Learning to cook with a variety of spices is a game changer in adding flavor to dishes! At first, this dish looks like it involves a lot of ingredients, but it is so simple to throw together and leave to simmer, all while packing a nutritional punch.

SERVES: **2**	YIELD: **3 CUPS**	PREP TIME: **10 MINUTES**	COOK TIME: **25 MINUTES**

TAGINE

2 tablespoons extra virgin olive oil

1 yellow onion, diced

2 garlic cloves, grated

1 teaspoon cumin seeds

1 tablespoon harissa paste

1 inch of fresh ginger root, grated

1 teaspoon ground cumin

1 teaspoon ground turmeric

1 teaspoon ground cinnamon

1 medium eggplant, cubed

1 medium zucchini, cut into 1-inch pieces

1 red bell pepper, sliced in strips

One 14-ounce (400 grams) can crushed tomatoes, with liquid

½ cup vegetable stock

1 pinch unrefined sea salt and pepper

One 14-ounce (400 grams) can garbanzo beans, drained and rinsed

¼ cup raisins

RAITA

1 small cucumber, diced

1 garlic clove, grated

2 tablespoons coconut yogurt

1 teaspoon ground turmeric

1 pinch unrefined sea salt

1. Heat the oil in a large saucepan over medium heat.

2. After 1 minute, add the onion, garlic, and cumin seeds and stir until the onion is almost translucent, about 3 minutes. Add the harissa paste, ginger, cumin, turmeric, and cinnamon, and cook for a further couple of minutes.

3. Once the spices are fragrant, add the eggplant, zucchini, and bell pepper. Cook for 5 minutes, stirring occasionally and making sure the spices do not burn on the bottom of the saucepan. Add a small amount of water if this happens.

4. Add the tomatoes and vegetable stock to the saucepan, and season with salt and pepper.

(Continued)

5. Bring the tagine to a boil, then reduce to a simmer over low heat. Pop on a lid and let the vegetables cook for 15 minutes. Test the vegetables at the 15-minute mark. If they're still firm, allow the vegetables to cook for a further 5 to 10 minutes.

6. Add the garbanzo beans and raisins and cook for 2 to 3 more minutes. Remove from the heat.

7. While the tagine is simmering, combine the raita ingredients and set aside.

8. Serve the tagine with a dollop of raita.

SWEET POTATO GNOCCHI WITH CREAMY GARLIC MUSHROOM SAUCE

Our sweet potato gnocchi requires a little more prep time than most dishes in this book, but it is well worth it and a fun one to learn on a weekend with the family!

SERVES: **2**	YIELD: **3 CUPS**	PREP TIME: **30 MINUTES**	COOK TIME: **30 MINUTES**

SWEET POTATO GNOCCHI

1 medium sweet potato, peeled and cut into chunks

1 cup cassava flour

1 organic free-range egg

CREAMY GARLIC MUSHROOM SAUCE

1 tablespoon extra virgin olive oil

1 spring onion, chopped

1 garlic clove, minced

1 anchovy

1 cup Swiss brown or cremini mushrooms, sliced

1 cup baby spinach leaves

½ cup coconut cream

1 pinch unrefined sea salt

2 tablespoons Brazil Nut Parmesan (page 215)

1. Cook the sweet potato in a pot of salted boiling water for 10 to 12 minutes, or until tender. Drain and allow to cool slightly.

2. Mash the sweet potato until smooth and free from lumps. Transfer to a large mixing bowl or a clean, floured work surface.

3. Mix ¾ cup of the cassava flour with the sweet potato. Make a well in the center and crack the egg into the well. Using your hands, combine the mixture.

4. If the sweet potato dough is too sticky, add a little more flour and continue kneading until a big dough ball is formed.

5. Slice the dough into quarters and roll each quarter into a 1-inch-wide rope. Then cut each rope into 1-inch gnocchi pieces.

6. To cook the gnocchi, bring a large pot of salted water to a boil. Add the gnocchi in batches and cook for 2 to 3 minutes or until the gnocchi float to the surface. Use a skimmer or slotted spoon to transfer the gnocchi to a large bowl.

7. To make the creamy garlic sauce, heat a large pan over medium-high heat. Add the oil and sauté the spring onion, garlic, and anchovy for 1 to 2 minutes.

(Continued)

8. Add the mushrooms and baby spinach and sauté for another 1 to 2 minutes. Stir in the coconut cream and mix well. Season with salt.

9. Mix the gnocchi into the mushroom mixture. Stir gently to coat well and serve with a sprinkle of Brazil Nut Parmesan.

FM TIP: The sweet potato gnocchi freezes well, so make it ahead of time for a quick midweek dinner without the prep. The gnocchi also goes well with our Hidden Vegetable Pasta Sauce (page 309).

FIJIAN COCONUT FISH CURRY

Shout-out to my parents for this recipe. Inspired from our time on the islands of Fiji, these flavors have made a way into our family recipes forever! — James

SERVES: **2**	YIELD: **3 CUPS**	PREP TIME: **5 MINUTES**	COOK TIME: **20 MINUTES**

1 tablespoon extra virgin olive oil

1 yellow onion, diced

1 long red chili, deseeded

1 inch of fresh ginger root, peeled and grated

1 garlic clove, minced

½ cup cilantro (coriander), stems and leaves separated

1 teaspoon ground turmeric

1 teaspoon ground cumin

1 pinch unrefined sea salt

1 handful green beans, sliced

1 medium carrot, thinly sliced

1 medium red bell pepper, thinly sliced

One 14-ounce (400 milliliters) can coconut cream

1 tablespoon tamari

Two 5-to-7-ounce (150 to 200 grams) fillets of white fish (snapper, barramundi, mahi mahi)

Juice of 1 lime

1 cup brown basmati rice, uncooked

1. Heat the oil in a large saucepan over medium heat. Add the onion and sauté for 5 minutes or until almost translucent.

2. Add the chili, ginger, garlic, cilantro stems, turmeric, cumin, and a pinch of salt. Cook for a further 5 minutes, stirring occasionally.

3. Once the spices are fragrant, add the green beans, carrot, and bell pepper and cook for a further 5 minutes.

4. Add the coconut cream, ½ cup water, and the tamari. Reduce to a simmer, cover with a lid, and cook for 10 minutes.

5. Cut the fish fillets into thirds and add to the curry. Cook for 5 minutes. Add the lime juice and cilantro leaves. Stir through.

6. Combine the rice with 2 cups water in a medium saucepan and bring to a boil. Stir once, cover with a tight-fitting lid, and reduce the heat to low. Simmer for 20 minutes. (Do not lift the lid or stir.) Remove from the heat and let stand, covered, for 5 minutes. Fluff with a fork.

7. Divide the fish curry into two servings and serve over the rice.

SPINACH, SWEET POTATO & LENTIL DAHL

Sometimes there is nothing more satisfying than a soul-warming bowl of comfort food, especially in the cooler months. This is a winter classic, packed with fresh, seasonal vegetables and spices to support digestion and immunity.

SERVES: **2**	YIELD: **4 CUPS**	PREP TIME: **10 MINUTES**	COOK TIME: **30 MINUTES**

1 tablespoon extra virgin olive oil

1 small yellow onion, finely diced

1 garlic clove, crushed

1 inch of fresh ginger root, peeled and finely chopped

½ long red chili, finely chopped

1 teaspoon ground turmeric

½ teaspoon ground cumin

½ teaspoon garam masala

1 tablespoon tomato paste

One 14-ounce (400 grams) can diced tomatoes, with liquid

1 medium sweet potato, cut into 1-inch chunks

½ cup red split lentils, soaked overnight

1 cup vegetable stock

Half a 14-ounce (400 milliliters) can coconut cream

1 cup baby spinach leaves

¼ cup cilantro (coriander) leaves

4 tablespoons coconut yogurt

1. Heat the oil in a large, wide-base pot or pan over medium-high heat. Add the onion and sauté for 1 to 2 minutes or until it begins to soften.

2. Add the garlic, ginger, and chili, continuing to sauté for another minute. Then add the turmeric, cumin, and garam masala. Lightly sauté for 2 to 3 minutes or until fragrant.

3. Add the tomato paste, tomatoes, sweet potato, lentils, stock, and coconut cream. Stir well and bring to a boil. Reduce heat to low and simmer for 20 to 25 minutes or until the sweet potato is cooked. Stir in the baby spinach right at the end.

4. Serve topped with the cilantro leaves and a dollop of coconut yogurt.

FM TIP: Soak your lentils overnight to help remove the phytic acid, making them easier to digest.

MUSHROOM & LENTIL BOLOGNESE WITH ZUCCHINI SPAGHETTI

Pasta can often leave you feeling heavy and bloated. One of the easiest solutions is to switch out traditional pasta for zucchini noodles. The hearty flavors of the mushroom and lentil bolognese will have you so satisfied you won't even notice the missing pasta.

| SERVES: 2 | YIELD. **4 CUPS** | PREP TIME: **25 MINUTES** | COOK TIME: **30 MINUTES** |

1 tablespoon extra virgin olive oil

1 carrot, diced

1 onion, diced

1 celery stalk, diced

2 garlic cloves, crushed

2 bay leaves

½ bunch thyme leaves

4 portobello mushrooms, stems removed and finely diced

½ cup red split lentils, soaked overnight

2 tablespoons tomato paste

One 14-ounce (400 grams) can diced tomatoes, with liquid

1 cup vegetable stock

½ teaspoon unrefined sea salt

½ teaspoon black pepper

⅓ cup fresh basil leaves

2 zucchini, spiralized

1. Add the oil to a medium pan over medium heat, and sauté the carrot, onion, celery, and garlic.

2. Add the bay leaves and thyme, stirring for 1 to 2 minutes or until soft.

3. Add the mushrooms and cook for 3 minutes, until softened.

4. Stir in the lentils, tomato paste, tomatoes, and stock.

5. Season with salt and pepper, reduce heat to low, and pop on a lid. Cook, stirring occasionally, for 15 to 20 minutes, or until the lentils are tender.

6. Stir the basil into the bolognese.

7. Bring a large pot of water to boil and blanch zucchini noodles for 3 minutes. Strain and serve with bolognese.

FM TIP: Using spiralized zucchini is a simple way to switch out gluten pasta. You'll be getting an extra serving of vegetables into your diet, and you'll feel a lot more energized.

ONE-TRAY MISO SALMON

Dinner doesn't need to be complicated to be nourishing! Nor do you need to use every dish in the house to create something delicious. There is nothing we love more midweek than a one-tray dinner!

SERVES: 2	YIELD: **2 SERVINGS**	PREP TIME: **25 MINUTES**	COOK TIME: **30 MINUTES**

½ **garlic clove, minced**

1 inch of fresh ginger root, grated

1 tablespoon white miso

1 teaspoon sesame oil

Two 5-to-7-ounce (150 to 200 grams) fillets of salmon

1 small sweet potato, cut into small cubes

1 tablespoon extra virgin olive oil

1 pinch unrefined sea salt and black pepper

1 cup broccoli florets

1 teaspoon sesame seeds

1. Preheat the oven to 350°F (180°C) and line a baking sheet with parchment paper.

2. Combine the garlic, ginger, miso, and sesame oil in a bowl. Add the salmon and coat. Set aside.

3. Place the sweet potato on the baking sheet, drizzle with the olive oil, and season with salt and pepper. Roast in the oven for 10 minutes.

4. After 10 minutes, add the salmon and broccoli to the same tray as the sweet potato. Continue roasting everything together for a further 15 minutes or until the salmon is cooked to your liking and the sweet potato is cooked through.

5. Serve topped with sesame seeds.

FM TIP: If animal products are in your diet, a healthy serving of fish is one of the best things you can have on your plate. Fish is a high-protein food, especially important for its omega-3 fatty acids. It is important to try to choose a sustainable choice. We have a full guide on FoodMatters.com on how to choose the best fish.

CLEAN FISH & CHIPS

This is our favorite way to make the most of freshly caught fish, without the nasties of a commercial deep fryer. If you've been looking for a new way to healthify this family-friendly classic, discover our must-try method for the best fish and chips you'll ever taste.

SERVES: **2**   YIELD: **2 SERVINGS**   PREP TIME: **10 MINUTES**   COOK TIME: **30 MINUTES**

1 small sweet potato, cut into wedges

2 tablespoons extra virgin olive oil, divided

2 pinches unrefined sea salt and black pepper, or to taste, divided

¼ cup tapioca flour

1 teaspoon lemon zest

Two 5-to-7-ounce (150 to 200 grams) firm white fish fillet (mahi mahi, snapper, or barramundi)

1 medium cucumber, diced

¼ red onion, finely sliced

1 baby romaine lettuce head, roughly chopped

Best Paleo Mayonnaise (page 223), to taste

½ lemon

1. Preheat the oven to 350°F (180°C).

2. Evenly place the potato wedges on a baking sheet lined with parchment paper. Drizzle with 1 tablespoon oil and season with a pinch of salt and pepper. Bake for 20 to 30 minutes until crisp and golden brown.

3. While the chips are baking, mix the tapioca flour, lemon zest, and a pinch of salt and pepper in a small bowl.

4. Coat both sides of each fillet evenly in the flour mixture. Set aside.

5. Heat 1 tablespoon oil in a frying pan over medium heat and pan-fry the fish for about 3 minutes on each side.

6. Toss the cucumber, red onion, and lettuce in a medium bowl.

7. Serve the fish with the crispy, oven-baked chips, the simple green salad, a side of the Best Paleo Mayonnaise, and a squeeze of lemon.

ONE-TRAY GREEK FISH BAKE

This One-Tray Greek Fish Bake brings together some amazing flavors from our travels, along with a healthy dose of omega-3 fatty acids and an array of nutrients.

SERVES: 2	YIELD: 2 SERVINGS	PREP: 5 MINUTES	COOKING TIME: 30 MINUTES

Zest and juice of 1 lemon

2 garlic cloves, crushed

½ teaspoon dried thyme

½ teaspoon dried oregano

2 ¼ teaspoons extra virgin olive oil, divided

½ teaspoon unrefined sea salt

½ teaspoon black pepper

Two 5-to-7-ounce (150 to 200 grams) fillets white fish (barramundi or mahi mahi)

1 red onion, cut into wedges

1 medium sweet potato, cubed

2 handfuls green beans (7 ounces), sliced in half

¼ bunch parsley, chopped

1 lemon

1. Preheat the oven to 350°F (180°C).

2. Combine the lemon zest, lemon juice, garlic, thyme, oregano, 1 ½ teaspoons oil, salt, and pepper in a bowl, and coat the fish fillets. Set aside for 15 minutes.

3. Coat the red onion and sweet potatoes with ¾ teaspoon oil, salt, and pepper in a baking dish. Roast in the oven for 15 minutes.

4. Add the fish and bake for a further 10 minutes. If your fish fillet is thicker than 1 inch, add an extra 5 minutes to the cooking time.

5. Scatter the green beans around the fish and bake for a further 5 minutes.

6. Serve the fish with the vegetables, topped with parsley and a squeeze of lemon juice.

TAMARI TUNA POKE BOWL

The now popular poke bowl originates from Hawaii, where *poke* means "to cut." Traditionally made from a combination of raw fish, rice, and vegetables, this dish now comes in many different varieties internationally.

SERVING SIZE: **2**   YIELD: **2 BOWLS**   PREP TIME: **10 MINUTES**   COOK TIME: **10 MINUTES**

---

3 tablespoons tamari

2 tablespoons pure maple syrup

½ inch of fresh ginger root, grated

2 tablespoons rice wine vinegar

¼ teaspoon red chili flakes

1 teaspoon sesame oil

1 cup quinoa, cooked

10 ounces (300 grams) sashimi-grade tuna, cubed

¼ head red cabbage, thinly sliced

1 carrot, julienned or thinly sliced

1 small mango

½ avocado, sliced

1 teaspoon sesame seeds

2 scallions, thinly sliced

1 tablespoon paleo mayonnaise (optional)

1. Mix the tamari, maple syrup, ginger, rice wine vinegar, chili flakes, and sesame oil to make the dressing. Set aside.

2. Assemble by dividing the quinoa into two bowls, topping each with the tuna, cabbage, carrot, mango, and avocado.

3. Top each bowl with the dressing, a sprinkle of sesame seeds, scallions, and paleo mayonnaise.

FM TIP: Not ready to try raw fish? Try lightly pan-frying your tuna for your bowl!

HEALTHY TACOS DONE 3 WAYS

If you were to ask us, "If you could only choose one, which food could you eat for the rest of your life?" our answer would be TACOS! We love them in every variety, especially these quick, simple, healthy, and delicious versions.

CRUNCHY CAULIFLOWER TACOS WITH ZESTY SLAW

SERVES: **2**   YIELD: **6 TACOS**   PREP TIME: **5 MINUTES**   COOK TIME: **25 MINUTES**

1 small head cauliflower, cut into bite-sized pieces

1 teaspoon chili powder

1 teaspoon sweet smoked paprika

1 teaspoon ground cumin

¼ cup tapioca flour

1 tablespoon extra virgin olive oil

2 pinches unrefined sea salt and black pepper, to taste, divided

½ small head red cabbage, thinly sliced

Juice of 1 lime

½ teaspoon apple cider vinegar

4 to 6 tortillas or Homemade Gluten-Free Wraps (page 220)

1 avocado, peeled and sliced

1. Preheat the oven to 350°F (180°C) and line a baking sheet with parchment paper.

2. Toss together the cauliflower, chili powder, paprika, cumin, tapioca flour, and oil in a large bowl, coating well. Season with a pinch of salt and pepper.

3. Assemble an even layer of the cauliflower on the baking sheet and bake for 20 minutes, or until golden brown and crisp.

4. While the cauliflower is baking, prepare the zesty slaw by combining the cabbage, lime juice, apple cider vinegar, and a pinch of salt and pepper in a bowl.

5. Assemble your tacos by piling your tortillas with the cauliflower and zesty slaw, then topping them with avocado.

EVERYDAY CHILI LIME FISH TACOS

SERVES: 2	YIELD: **6 TACOS**	PREP TIME: **15 MINUTES**	COOK TIME: **20 MINUTES**

3 tablespoons extra virgin olive oil

Juice of 2 limes, divided

1 teaspoon chili powder

1 garlic clove, crushed

2 pinches unrefined sea salt, to taste, divided

Two 5-ounce (150 grams) fillets white fish (barramundi or mahi mahi)

1 mango, fresh or frozen, diced

½ cup cilantro, roughly chopped

¼ red onion, thinly diced

¼ bunch (about 4) radishes, diced

1 long red chili, deseeded, thinly sliced

4 to 6 tortillas or Homemade Gluten-Free Wraps (page 220)

½ avocado, sliced

1. Preheat the oven to 400°F (200°C).

2. Whisk together the oil, juice of one lime, chili powder, garlic, and a pinch of salt in a bowl.

3. Pour the dressing over the fish in an oven-proof dish. Bake for 15 to 20 minutes.

4. While the fish is baking, prepare the salsa by mixing the mango, cilantro, onion, radishes, chili, juice of ½ a lime, and a pinch of salt in a bowl. Set aside.

5. Layer the tortillas with the fish, salsa, avocado, and a squeeze of lime.

VEGAN CARNITAS WITH JACKFRUIT & MUSHROOM

SERVES: **2**　　　　YIELD: **6 TACOS**　　　　PREP TIME: **15 MINUTES**　　　　COOK TIME: **20 MINUTES**

1 small red onion, thinly sliced

2 garlic cloves, crushed

1 cup button mushrooms, thinly sliced

One 14-ounce (400 grams) can of young jackfruit, drained, rinsed, and sliced

2 tablespoons extra virgin olive oil, divided

Juice of 1 ½ limes, divided

1 tablespoon tamari

1 teaspoon ground cumin

2 teaspoons ground coriander

1 teaspoon smoked paprika

1 teaspoon dried oregano

4 to 6 tortillas or Homemade Gluten-Free Wraps (page 220)

½ avocado, sliced

¼ small head red cabbage, finely shredded

Handful of fresh cilantro (coriander)

1. Combine the onion, garlic, mushrooms, and jackfruit in a large bowl. Coat with 1 tablespoon oil, the juice of 1 lime, and tamari. Mix well and set aside to marinate for 10 minutes.

2. Combine the cumin, coriander, paprika, and oregano in a small bowl. Set aside.

3. Add 1 tablespoon oil to a large frying pan over medium-high heat, followed by the marinated mushroom-jackfruit mix. Cook for 10 to 12 minutes or until the mushrooms begin to soften.

4. Add the spice mix, stirring well to coat all the ingredients. Continue to cook for 1 to 2 minutes.

5. Assemble the tacos by layering the tortillas with the mushroom-jackfruit mixture, avocado, cabbage, fresh cilantro, and a squeeze of lime.

GLUTEN-FREE PIZZA WITH SEASONAL ROAST VEG

There's something so satisfying about making a homemade pizza! Our gluten-free base is easy to put together and bakes nicely with any of your favorite pizza toppings. We love using whatever is in season.

SERVES: 2	YIELD: 2 PIZZAS	PREP TIME: 20 MINUTES	COOK TIME: 25 MINUTES

PIZZA DOUGH

1 ½ cups cassava flour

1 cup tapioca flour

2 teaspoons unrefined sea salt

1 teaspoon dried oregano

1 teaspoon dried thyme

2 organic free-range eggs

½ cup olive oil, plus more for oiling dough

1 cup water, room temperature

TOPPINGS

¼ cup Hidden Vegetable Pasta Sauce (page 309)

1 small zucchini, grated into ribbons

½ red onion, thinly sliced

½ red bell pepper, thinly sliced

¼ cup kalamata olives, pitted and halved

3 tablespoons Cashew Hemp Basil Pesto (page 208)

Handful of fresh basil leaves

1. Preheat the oven to 400°F (200°C). Though not necessary, if you have a pizza stone, place it in the oven to heat.

2. Combine the cassava flour, tapioca flour, salt, oregano, and thyme in a medium mixing bowl. Create a well in the center.

3. Add the eggs, oil, and ½ cup water to the center of the well. Fold the mixture to combine all the ingredients well, gradually adding more water as needed. You want the mixture to be sticky enough to roll out.

4. Chill the dough in the refrigerator or freezer for around 20 minutes while you prepare the pizza toppings. This will allow the dough to firm up and make it easier to handle.

5. Place a piece of parchment paper on your work surface and coat your hands in a small amount of oil to prevent dough from sticking.

6. Scoop out the dough and divide in half. Form each half into a ball. Use a rolling pin or glass bottle to roll out each ball as thinly as possible.

7. Bake on a pizza stone or baking tray for 10 minutes or until the base begins to brown.

8. Remove from the oven and top with the pasta sauce, zucchini, onion, pepper, olives, and pesto.

9. Return to the oven and bake for another 15 minutes until the vegetables are just browned and the crust is done to your liking. Top with basil and serve.

FM TIP: Some of our favorite topping variations include: any leftover roast vegetables from throughout the week, roast pumpkin, caramelized onions, goat cheese, and mushrooms.

SUPER GREEN PESTO PASTA

Struggling to get extra greens into your diet? Dark leafy greens and vegetables are some of the most nutrient-dense foods we can eat, but some days it can be harder than others to get in our greens! This Super Green Pesto Pasta is packed with flavor (and extra greens), but you won't even think about that when you're eating it.

SERVES: **2**   YIELD: **3 CUPS**   PREP TIME: **10 MINUTES**   COOK TIME: **15 MINUTES**

KALE AND BROCCOLI PESTO

1 cup Tuscan kale leaves, stems removed

1 head broccoli, cut into florets

1 cup basil leaves

2 tablespoons pepitas

2 tablespoons nutritional yeast

Zest and juice of 1 lemon

1 garlic clove, crushed

¼ teaspoon crushed chili flakes (optional)

2 tablespoons extra virgin olive oil

½ teaspoon unrefined sea salt

½ teaspoon black pepper

PASTA

1 cup brown rice pasta

2 tablespoons pepitas

1 tablespoon extra virgin olive oil

1 small zucchini, cut into thin ribbons

2 cups leafy greens, such as arugula

1 to 2 tablespoons Brazil Nut Parmesan (page 215, optional)

1. Blitz the kale, broccoli, basil, pepitas, nutritional yeast, lemon juice, lemon zest, garlic, chili flakes (if using), oil, salt, and pepper in a food processor until well combined. If you prefer, you can keep it a little chunky for texture.

2. In a medium saucepan, boil enough salted water to cover the pasta. Cook the pasta as per the package instructions.

3. While the pasta is cooking, lightly toast the pepitas in a frying pan over medium heat until they begin to brown and pop; this will only take about 30 to 60 seconds. Transfer the pepitas to a small bowl. Return the pan to medium heat, add the oil, and lightly fry the zucchini.

4. Once the pasta is cooked, drain and add to the zucchini, along with the kale and broccoli pesto. Toss all the ingredients to ensure the pasta is coated well.

5. Toss in the leafy greens and mix thoroughly. Top with the toasted pepitas and Brazil Nut Parmesan to serve.

FM TIP: There are some tasty gluten-free pasta options on the market now. One of our favorites is brown rice pasta, which has a mild, chewy texture and is a great source of fiber.

TRAY BAKE JACKFRUIT NACHOS WITH CHARRED CORN SALSA

A healthy fast-food swap that tastes better than you can imagine! This crowd-pleasing dish is meant to be shared.

SERVES: **4**   YIELD: **1 LARGE TRAY OR 4 SERVINGS**   PREP TIME: **20 MINUTES**   COOK TIME: **15 MINUTES**

CHARRED CORN SALSA

1 cob of corn, shucked

2 teaspoons extra virgin olive oil

½ red onion, finely diced

1 tomato, finely diced

¼ cup cilantro (coriander), roughly chopped

1 pinch unrefined sea salt

Juice of ½ lime

JACKFRUIT CHILI

1 tablespoon extra virgin olive oil

1 tablespoon smoked paprika

½ red onion, finely chopped

1 small red bell pepper, deseeded and diced

1 red chili, finely chopped, deseeded if preferred

1 tablespoon cilantro (coriander) stems, finely chopped

One 14-ounce (400 grams) can young jackfruit, drained and rinsed

One 14-ounce (400 grams) can diced tomatoes, with liquid

One 14-ounce (400 grams) can black beans, drained and rinsed

½ teaspoon unrefined sea salt

GUACAMOLE

1 large or 2 small avocados, halved and seed removed

Juice of ½ lime

1 pinch unrefined sea salt and black pepper

One 11-ounce (300 grams) bag of organic corn chips

(Continued)

1. Preheat the oven to 400°F (200°C) and line a baking tray with parchment paper.

2. To prepare the salsa, lightly coat the corn cob in 2 teaspoons of oil before adding to a frying pan over medium-high heat. Continue turning to cook evenly for 4 to 5 minutes until the corn is slightly charred. You could also do this on a naked flame if you are confident and have access to one. Remove from the heat and allow to cool before cutting off the kernels. Mix the corn with the onion, tomato, cilantro, salt, and lime juice, and set aside.

3. Add 1 tablespoon of oil to the same pan over medium heat, followed by the paprika, onion, bell pepper, chili, and cilantro stems. Fry 1 to 2 minutes until the mixture softens and smells fragrant. Add the jackfruit, tomatoes, beans, and salt, stir well, and simmer for 5 minutes or until liquid has reduced. Remove from the heat.

4. To prepare the guacamole, mash the avocados with a fork in a bowl, then add the lime juice, salt, and pepper. Mix well.

5. To assemble the nachos, layer the corn chips on the baking tray and top with the jackfruit chili. Bake for 10 minutes or until the corn chips begin to brown.

6. Serve topped with the charred corn salsa and guacamole.

MUSHROOM MISO RAMEN

Japanese food is always inspiring with its flavors, presentation, and colors. Miso is a common ingredient, and when you choose a traditionally fermented miso, you will get the most out of its health benefits. Rich in amino acids, miso helps to stimulate the digestive system and store the good gut bacteria.

SERVES: **2**	YIELD: **4 CUPS**	PREP TIME: **15 MINUTES**	COOK TIME: **30 MINUTES**

One 10-ounce (300 grams) package tempeh, sliced into thin pieces

2 tablespoons sesame oil, divided

3 tablespoons tamari, divided

3 garlic cloves, crushed, divided

3 inches of fresh ginger root, grated, divided

1 tablespoon pure maple syrup

Juice of 1 lime

1 yellow onion, diced

4 cups Restorative Vegetable or Bone Broth (page 272)

1 ounce dried shiitake mushrooms

2 tablespoons mirin

2 tablespoons dark miso

1 cup mixed mushrooms (shiitake, enoki, and oyster), thinly sliced

4 ounces brown rice noodles or kelp noodles

1 head bok choy, roughly chopped

2 spring onions, thinly sliced

1 tablespoon toasted sesame seeds

Sliced chili pepper or dried chili flakes to taste (optional)

1. Marinate the tempeh in 1 tablespoon sesame oil, 2 tablespoons tamari, 1 crushed garlic clove, 1 tablespoon ginger, maple syrup, and lime juice. Set aside.

2. To prepare the mushroom miso broth, add 1 tablespoon sesame oil in a large pot over medium-high heat, followed by the onion, and cook for around 2-3 minutes or until the onion softens and becomes translucent.

3. Add 2 crushed garlic cloves and 2 tablespoons ginger. Continue to sauté for 1 minute. Add the broth and dried mushrooms, cover, and bring to a boil.

4. Add 1 tablespoon tamari, mirin, and miso, stirring well, then reduce the heat and simmer for 20 minutes.

5. While the broth simmers, fry the tempeh in a small frying pan over medium heat until golden brown on the outside, about 1 to 2 minutes on each side. Remove from the heat and set the tempeh aside. Add the mushroom mixture to the same pan and fry with the leftover marinade. Remove from the heat and prepare the noodles according to the package instructions.

6. To serve, divide the mushroom miso broth and noodles between two deep bowls. Top with the tempeh, mushrooms, bok choy, spring onions, sesame seeds, and chili, if using.

FM TIP: For the tempeh to soak up extra flavor, marinate the night before.

ONE-POT
SATAY SOBA NOODLES

On the hunt for a quick and healthy noodle dish? With a few key ingredients, a flavor-packed sauce, and some good-quality noodles, you've got yourself a quick dinner that's sure to hit your craving!

| SERVES: **2** | YIELD: **3 CUPS** | PREP TIME: **15 MINUTES** | COOK TIME: **10 MINUTES** |

½ cup peanut or almond butter

¼ cup tamari

2 tablespoon rice wine vinegar

1 tablespoon pure maple syrup

1 inch of fresh ginger root, grated

1 garlic clove, crushed

6 ounces soba noodles or brown rice noodles

2 tablespoons extra virgin olive oil

1 bunch broccolini, roughly chopped

1 pinch unrefined sea salt

1 lime wedge

1 tablespoon toasted sesame seeds

1. Prepare the satay sauce by whisking together the nut butter, tamari, rice wine vinegar, maple syrup, ginger, garlic, and 2 tablespoons hot water in a bowl.

2. Bring a pot of water to a boil. Once boiling, cook the noodles for 7 to 8 minutes or until al dente. Drain the noodles and set them aside in a bowl.

3. Return the pot to medium heat and add oil. Add the broccolini and salt. Toss for 3 to 4 minutes or until cooked.

4. Transfer the noodles back into the pot with the broccolini, then stir through the nutty satay sauce until the noodles and broccolini are coated well.

5. Serve in bowls topped with a squeeze of lime juice and a sprinkle of toasted sesame seeds.

ONE-POT COCONUT CAULIFLOWER CURRY

This one-pot dish is the Food Matters vegan take on butter chicken. Loaded with nutrients and flavor from cauliflower and spices, it's easy to throw together and simmer!

SERVES: **4**	YIELD: **4 CUPS**	PREP TIME: **10 MINUTES**	COOK TIME: **25 MINUTES**

2 tablespoons extra virgin olive oil

1 small yellow onion, finely diced

3 garlic cloves, crushed

2 inches of fresh ginger root, grated

1 tablespoon garam masala

2 teaspoons curry powder

½ teaspoon ground turmeric

½ teaspoon cayenne pepper

¾ cup (6 ounces) tomato paste

2 tablespoons coconut oil

1 large head cauliflower, trimmed and cut into florets

One 14-ounce (400 milliliters) can coconut milk

1 cup steamed rice

¼ cup cilantro, roughly chopped

1. Sauté the oil and onion in a large frying pan over medium heat for 3 to 4 minutes or until the onion begins to become translucent.

2. Add the garlic and ginger, cooking for another 2 to 3 minutes or until fragrant. Add the garam masala, curry powder, turmeric, and cayenne. Cook for about 1 minute until fragrant.

3. Stir in the tomato paste and coconut oil. Add the cauliflower and toss to coat.

4. Add the coconut milk, stirring well, reduce the heat to low, and simmer for 20 to 25 minutes or until the cauliflower is cooked through.

5. Serve the cauliflower and sauce over a bowl of steamed rice, topped with cilantro.

ONE-PAN LEMONGRASS & COCONUT STEAMED FISH PARCELS

These Thai-inspired steamed fish parcels are a simple and satisfying midweek recipe with little prep and cook time.

SERVES: 2	YIELD: **2 PARCELS**	PREP TIME: **10 MINUTES**	COOK TIME: **20 MINUTES**

3 lemongrass stalks, halved

½ tablespoon grated fresh ginger

½ tablespoon tamari

2 teaspoons coconut sugar

Juice of 2 fresh limes

¼ cup (2 ounces) canned coconut milk

1 small zucchini, thinly sliced

1 small red bell pepper, deseeded and thinly sliced

Two 5-ounce (150 grams) fillets white fish (snapper, barramundi, or mahi mahi)

1 small head bok choy, roughly chopped

¼ cup cilantro leaves (optional)

1 red chili, thinly sliced (optional)

1. Preheat the oven to 400°F (200°C).

2. To prepare the dressing, trim the ends from the lemongrass, remove the outer layer, and use the back of your knife to carefully bruise the lemongrass by hitting the sticks on the chopping board. This helps to release the oils and fragrance of the lemongrass.

3. Mix the lemongrass, ginger, tamari, coconut sugar, lime juice, and coconut milk in a bowl and let sit while you prepare the fish.

4. To prepare the fish, take 2 large pieces of parchment paper big enough to encase your fish and chopped vegetables, and place them on a baking tray.

5. Divide the zucchini and red peppers in half between the two sheets of paper. Place a fillet of fish on top of each parcel, then top with the bok choy. Pour half of the dressing over each fish parcel.

6. Fold up the sides of the parchment paper, followed by both ends, scrunching and twisting together to seal the parcels.

7. Bake for 15 to 18 minutes. Remove from the oven and let sit for 5 minutes before opening the parcels. Remove the lemongrass stalks before serving. Serve with cilantro and chili.

ONE-PAN BAKED PESTO SALMON WITH ROOT VEGETABLES

This is one hearty, cozy dinner recipe for those cooler months. Use any seasonal veg to make the most of your local produce.

SERVES: 2	YIELD: **2 SERVINGS**	PREP TIME: **10 MINUTES**	COOK TIME: **35 MINUTES**

2 small beets, halved

2 carrots, chopped

1 small sweet potato, diced

6 brussels sprouts, halved

2 tablespoons extra virgin olive oil

½ teaspoon unrefined sea salt, or to taste

½ teaspoon black pepper, or to taste

¼ cup Cashew Hemp Basil Pesto (page 208)

Two 5-to-7-ounce (150 to 200 grams) salmon fillets

Juice of ½ lemon

1. Preheat the oven to 400°F (200°C).

2. On a lined baking tray, toss the beets, carrots, sweet potatoes, and brussels sprouts with oil, salt, and pepper. Roast for 20 minutes.

3. Make the hemp pesto if you haven't already.

4. Remove the vegetables from the oven, place the salmon fillets in the middle of the tray, and top with enough pesto to cover the top of the fillets.

5. Return to the oven and roast for 12 to 15 minutes, or until the salmon is cooked to your liking.

6. Serve the salmon with a squeeze of lemon juice and an extra dollop of pesto on the side.

DIPS, SIDES & STAPLES

CASHEW HEMP BASIL PESTO

Some things in life are worth holding on to, and that includes a good pesto recipe. Our version of basil pesto doesn't require any complicated ingredients, just whole-foods pantry staples and a whole lot of love.

SERVES: **4**	YIELD: **1 ½ CUPS**	PREP TIME: **5 MINUTES**	COOK TIME: **NONE**

1 cup basil leaves

1 garlic clove, peeled

¼ cup activated cashews

1 tablespoon hemp seeds

1 pinch unrefined sea salt and black pepper

¼ cup extra virgin olive oil

Juice of 1 lemon

1 tablespoon nutritional yeast (optional)

1. Blend all the ingredients in a food processor. If using a mortar and pestle, grind the basil, garlic, cashews, hemp seeds, salt, and pepper to form a paste. Add the oil and lemon juice at the end and mix. If you'd like a cheesier flavor, add nutritional yeast.

2. Store in an airtight container or jar in the fridge for up to 5 days.

FM TIP: The addition of hemp seeds provides a powerful nutrition punch, and the added yeast offers a traditional "cheesy" flavor, without the dairy. It's an all-around winner, and you'll find yourself making it weekly!

SALSA VERDE

This signature staple in our Clean Eating Program is a great addition to almost anything and a way to use a variety of green herbs with many amazing nutritional benefits.

SERVES: **4**   YIELD: **1 CUP**   PREP TIME: **10 MINUTES**   COOK TIME. **NONE**

1 garlic clove, peeled

1 cup basil

1 cup mint

1 tablespoon baby capers and brine

3 anchovy fillets

1 teaspoon Dijon mustard

1 tablespoon apple cider vinegar

2 tablespoons extra virgin olive oil

Juice of 1 lemon

1. Blend all the ingredients in a food processor or blender until combined.

2. Store in an airtight jar in the fridge for up to 5 days.

HOMEMADE HUMMUS

We've got a secret to share: homemade hummus is always 10 times better than any store-bought hummus, without the nasties! Using harissa or paprika adds an earthy, slightly spicy and smoky flavor.

SERVES: **4**   YIELD: **2 CUPS**   PREP TIME: **5 MINUTES**   COOKING TIME: **NONE**

One 14-ounce (400 grams) can garbanzo beans (chickpeas), rinsed and drained

2 tablespoons tahini

1 garlic clove, chopped

Juice of 1 lemon

2 teaspoons harissa paste or sweet smoked paprika

1 pinch unrefined sea salt and black pepper

1 to 3 tablespoons extra virgin olive oil

1. Blitz the garbanzo beans, tahini, garlic, lemon juice, harissa, salt, and pepper in a food processor or blender until smooth.

2. Turn the food processor or blender down to its slowest speed and add the oil slowly until a smooth consistency is achieved.

3. Store in an airtight container in the fridge for up to a week.

BRAZIL NUT PARMESAN

With just three ingredients, this staple is free from dairy but still offers that "cheesy" flavor to any dish. This game changer lasts in the pantry, so you can always keep a batch on hand!

SERVES: **8 TO 10**   YIELD: **1 CUP**   PREP TIME: **5 MINUTES**   COOK TIME: **NONE**

1 cup whole, raw, activated Brazil nuts

½ cup nutritional yeast

1 pinch unrefined sea salt

1. Blend the Brazil nuts, yeast, and salt in a food processor or blender until it forms a fine crumble.

2. Store in an airtight container or jar in the fridge for 2 to 3 weeks.

HOMEMADE GRANOLA

Most store-bought versions of granola contain the equivalent sugar levels of a chocolate cake for dessert! The good news is that you can create your own version at home. It will taste better, have a lot less sugar, and offer you more health benefits. It takes no time at all and makes your house smell amazing while it bakes.

| SERVES: **10** | YIELD: **3 CUPS** | PREP TIME: **10 MINUTES** | COOK TIME: **25 MINUTES** |

1 ½ cups instant gluten-free oats

½ cup coconut flakes

1 cup activated almonds, chopped

½ cup activated walnuts, chopped

1 tablespoon sesame seeds

½ teaspoon unrefined sea salt

3 tablespoons coconut oil

¼ cup pure maple syrup

1 teaspoon vanilla extract

½ teaspoon ground cardamom

½ teaspoon ground nutmeg

½ teaspoon ground cinnamon

1. Preheat the oven to 350°F (180°C) and line a baking sheet with parchment paper.

2. Mix the oats, coconut flakes, almonds, walnuts, sesame seeds, and salt in a large bowl.

3. Melt the oil, maple syrup, and vanilla extract in a small saucepan over low heat along with the cardamom, nutmeg, and cinnamon. Stir for about 2 minutes.

4. Pour the maple syrup mixture over the oat mixture. Spread the granola evenly on the parchment-lined baking sheet.

5. Bake for 25 minutes, or until golden brown.

6. Set aside to cool for 10 minutes without stirring. This will help the granola to set crunchy.

7. Break apart the crunchy granola. Store in an airtight container for up to 1 month.

GOLDEN TURMERIC PASTE

Curcumin, the main compound responsible for turmeric's anti-inflammatory benefits, is very quickly metabolized and not well absorbed by the body at all. Piperine, the compound responsible for the heat of black pepper, helps slow the liver from metabolizing curcumin too quickly. Coconut oil or other fats also help to slow down this process.

SERVES: **10**	YIELD: **1 CUP**	PREP TIME: **5 MINUTES**	COOK TIME: **5 MINUTES**

½ cup organic turmeric powder, plus more to adjust consistency

¼ cup extra virgin coconut oil or other fat, such as ghee or extra virgin olive oil

1 teaspoon black pepper

1 to 2 tablespoons raw honey (optional)

1 to 2 teaspoons warming spices, such as ground nutmeg, curry powder, cinnamon, and cardamom (optional)

1 to 2 teaspoons unrefined sea salt (optional)

1. Add the turmeric and 1 cup filtered water to a small pan on low to medium-low heat for 3 to 4 minutes or until it begins to form a thick paste.

2. Add the oil and black pepper and combine well, adjusting the water or turmeric as needed to keep a thick, paste-like consistency.

3. Add 1 to 2 tablespoons of raw honey and 1 to 2 teaspoons of salt or warming spices such as nutmeg, curry powder, cinnamon, and cardamom (all of which pair well with turmeric), if you wish.

4. Once your paste is the consistency you desire, store it in a glass jar with a tight-fitting lid in the refrigerator for 1 to 2 months.

5. Dilute and consume 1 to 2 teaspoons of paste a day in warm water, juices, smoothies, teas, golden milk, nut butter, stir-fries, soups, stews, dressings, and other savory items.

HOMEMADE GLUTEN-FREE WRAPS

These gluten-free wraps are a staple throughout this book and in our signature Clean Eating Program. They are super easy to make, filling, and make a great replacement for store-bought wraps and tortillas.

SERVES: **1**	YIELD: **4 TO 6 WRAPS** (MAKES 4 LARGE OR 6 TO 8 SMALL)	PREP TIME: **2 MINUTES**	COOK TIME: **5 MINUTES**

1 cup almond meal

1 cup tapioca flour

2 organic free-range eggs

½ cup (4 ounces) canned coconut milk

1 pinch unrefined sea salt

1 teaspoon coconut oil

1. Combine the almond meal, tapioca flour, eggs, coconut milk, ½ cup water, and salt in a bowl to form a smooth, thin batter. You may need to add a little more water to thin out the mixture.

2. Melt the coconut oil in a small frying pan over medium heat.

3. Ladle ¼ cup batter into the pan, tilting and swirling to coat the base in an even layer. When using the recipe for taco tortillas, you might want to use a little less batter at a time to make small taco wraps.

4. Cook for 2 to 3 minutes, then carefully turn the wrap over with a spatula and cook for a further 2 minutes, or until golden. Lift the wrap from the pan and set aside.

5. Repeat with the remaining mixture, greasing the pan with more coconut oil as needed between wraps.

FM TIP: For an equally delicious wrap, you can use 2 cups of manioc/cassava flour instead of the almond-and-tapioca flour mix.

BEST PALEO MAYONNAISE

Mayonnaise is a favorite condiment in many households. While traditional mayonnaise was once made with only a few ingredients, it's now hard to find a product that doesn't have added preservatives and cheap vegetable oils. This version is made from whole-food ingredients, so you can eat knowing you are also receiving health benefits.

SERVES: **10**	YIELD: **1 CUP**	PREP TIME: **15 MINUTES**	COOK TIME: **NONE**

3 yolks from organic free-range eggs

¼ teaspoon ground mustard

1 teaspoon unrefined sea salt, or to taste, divided

1 tablespoon apple cider vinegar

¾ to 1 cup avocado oil

1 pinch black pepper

1. Add the egg yolks, mustard, ½ teaspoon salt, and apple cider vinegar in a large jar or large mixing bowl.

2. Blend, using an immersion blender or whisk, on high until mixed well.

3. Gradually pour in the avocado oil as you continue to mix. This helps the emulsification process.

4. Taste and adjust the flavor using a pinch of salt and pepper.

RASPBERRY CHIA SEED JAM

Four ingredients and five minutes is all it takes to make one of our favorite condiments!

SERVES: **10** YIELD: **1 CUP** PREP TIME: **5 MINUTES** COOK TIME: **5 MINUTES**

---

2 cups raspberries, fresh or frozen

1 tablespoon pure maple syrup

¼ cup chia seeds

Juice of 1 lemon

1. Stir the raspberries and 2 tablespoons of water in a small saucepan over medium heat until the fruit softens, breaks down, and gently simmers. Mash the raspberries with a fork or vegetable masher.

2. Add the maple syrup, chia seeds, and lemon juice. Stir until combined, then remove from heat.

3. Allow to cool. The jam will thicken as the mixture cools.

4. Serve immediately or store in an airtight container in the refrigerator for up to 1 week.

SUN-DRIED TOMATO & CHICKPEA QUICK DIP

Rich in flavor and nutrients, this quick dip will soon become one of your favorite weekly must-haves!

SERVES: **4**	YIELD: **2 CUPS**	PREP TIME: **5 MINUTES**	COOK TIME. **NONE**

One 14-ounce (400 grams) can chickpeas, drained and rinsed

½ cup sun-dried tomatoes in extra virgin olive oil, roughly chopped

2 tablespoons extra virgin olive oil

Juice of 1 lemon

2 tablespoons tahini

2 garlic cloves, crushed

½ teaspoon unrefined sea salt

¼ cup fresh basil leaves, roughly chopped

1. Process the chickpeas, sun-dried tomatoes, oil, lemon juice, tahini, garlic, and salt in a food processor or high-powered blender until you reach a smooth consistency.

2. Add the basil and pulse 1 to 2 times, until the basil is just mixed through.

3. Serve immediately or store in the refrigerator for up to a week.

FM TIP: This dip is best served with our Rosemary & Sea Salt Cassava Crackers (page 327) for the ultimate healthy snack!

HOMEMADE SALAD DRESSINGS

Forget the store-bought salad dressings! They're typically loaded with emulsifiers, stabilizers, artificial flavors, and other unnecessary additives. Make these savory ones instead; they'll transform your everyday salad into a taste sensation!

MISO-GINGER DRESSING

1 tablespoon white miso

2 tablespoons pure maple syrup

1 inch of fresh ginger root, grated

2 tablespoons extra virgin olive oil

¼ cup apple cider vinegar

LEMON TAHINI DRESSING

¼ cup tahini

Juice of 1 lemon

¼ cup extra virgin olive oil

1 garlic clove, crushed

1 tablespoon pure maple syrup or honey

Unrefined sea salt and black pepper, to taste

TAMARI ASIAN DRESSING

1 tablespoon tamari

Juice of ½ lime

1 tablespoon rice wine vinegar

1 ½ teaspoons sesame seeds

1 teaspoon sesame oil

SATAY DRESSING

½ cup nut butter

1 inch of fresh ginger root, grated

1 garlic clove, crushed

2 tablespoons

coconut sugar

2 tablespoons tamari

¼ cup coconut milk

Juice of 1 lime

Whisk all the ingredients together until well blended. Store in jars with tight lids. These will last in the refrigerator for up to one month.

HERBY AVOCADO DRESSING

2 avocados, peeled and deseeded

¼ cup loosely packed fresh herbs (basil, parsley, cilantro, and thyme)

1 garlic clove, crushed

Juice of 1 lemon

OUR FAVORITE FERMENTS

SIMPLE SAUERKRAUT

Sauerkraut was said to have originated in China more than 2,000 years ago and was later brought to Europe. It could, perhaps, be one of the most vital things you could add to your diet. To nourish your gut is to nourish your body. Sauerkraut works wonders for your digestion, producing amazing amounts of probiotics. The fermentation also produces isothiocyanates, compounds shown to prevent disease.[9] The cabbage itself contains similar anticarcinogenic phytochemicals as broccoli and brussels sprouts, and is also a good source of vitamins C and K and folate.

2 medium cabbages, red or green, or one of each (approx. 2.5 to 3 pounds total), cored

3 tablespoons unrefined sea salt

2 tablespoons caraway seeds (optional)

SPECIAL EQUIPMENT

1.5-to-2-quart wide-mouth mason jar or ceramic pot, with lid

1. Thinly slice the cabbage using a food processor or good knife. Place in a large bowl and add the salt and, if using, the caraway seeds.

2. Mix with your hands, squeezing firmly and pushing down the cabbage with your fist to encourage the salt to draw out the natural water. Continue to do this for the next 15 minutes or so. You want to extract enough of the cabbages' juices so that they will cover the cabbage when it goes in the jar or pot.

3. Transfer the cabbage to the jar, along with all the liquid to submerge the cabbage. (If there's not enough juice, add water.)

4. Cover with a lid or tea towel and leave at room temperature in a dark corner of your kitchen for 1 to 3 weeks (less time in summer, longer in winter). It's ready when it tastes sour and tangy and the cabbage has become soft.

5. Once sufficiently fermented, seal and store in the refrigerator. It will last 12 months unopened, and 2 months once opened.

    FM TIP: Once opened, keep refrigerated. Keep veggies submerged in their liquid and don't heat them.

CULTURED TOMATO KETCHUP

Did you know that, traditionally, tomato ketchup was a fermented product? Somewhere along the way, we were introduced to sugar-filled store-bought ketchup and sauces. If you're new to fermenting, then this recipe is a good place to start. It's quick and easy to make, has a subtle tang, and makes a superb addition to many dishes.

Two 6-ounce cans of tomato paste

3 tablespoons pure maple syrup

3 tablespoons apple cider vinegar, with the "mother"*

2 tablespoons brine from existing vegetable ferments

¼ teaspoon onion powder

½ teaspoon unrefined sea salt

¼ teaspoon black pepper

¼ teaspoon allspice

1. In a bowl, combine all the ingredients, mixing well and adjusting any seasonings to taste.

2. Transfer the mixture to a large mason jar and fit with a lid to ensure it is airtight.

3. Leave the ketchup out at room temperature for 2 to 3 days, depending on the season you are in (less time in summer, longer in winter).

4. "Burp" the ketchup every day or so by releasing the lid to release any buildup of gas.

5. Once the fermented ketchup is ready, store it in the refrigerator. You will know it's ready when it has a slightly tangy taste. If you like it tangier, let it ferment a little longer.

*For this recipe, use apple cider vinegar with "the active mother," live bacteria in the ACV that will assist with the natural fermentation process, available in most supermarkets and all health food stores.

FM TIP: Opt for an organic tomato paste when making this recipe and be sure to check out the ingredients. Many pastes are loaded with extra salt, which we should aim to avoid. This recipe makes a great bottled sauce replacement!

SALADS & SIDES

SKIN BEAUTY SALAD

Foods aren't just good for your insides; they make your outer layer shine too! Take our staple Skin Beauty Salad, which is rich in omega-3 fatty acids, a key ingredient in healthy skin and a radiant glow.

| SERVINGS: **2** | YIELD: **3 CUPS** | PREP TIME: **10 MINUTES** | COOK TIME: **NONE** |

½ avocado

1 tablespoon apple cider vinegar

Juice of 1 lime

¼ teaspoon cayenne pepper

1 teaspoon pure maple syrup

1 pinch unrefined sea salt

2 baby romaine lettuce heads, roughly chopped

1 carrot, diced

1 medium cucumber, diced

¼ cup radishes, diced

Half a 14-ounce (400 grams) can garbanzo beans (chickpeas)

¼ bunch parsley, roughly chopped

¼ bunch mint, roughly chopped

¼ red onion, finely diced

1 tablespoon hemp seeds

1. For the dressing, mash the avocado using a fork. Add the apple cider vinegar, lime juice, cayenne pepper, maple syrup, and salt, and stir until a smooth consistency is achieved. If you have a blender, you may prefer to use that.

2. In a large bowl, arrange the lettuce leaves, carrot, cucumber, radishes, garbanzo beans, parsley, mint, and onion.

3. Dollop the dressing generously on your salad. Mix through before eating. Garnish with the hemp seeds.

FM TIP: If you're not a fan of the strong flavor of the red onion, you can soak the onion in lime juice for 10 minutes while you're making the salad.

THAI QUINOA SALAD
WITH SPICY NUT DRESSING

Thai is one of those cuisines that we come back to time and time again. This fresh take on a salad is pad thai–inspired, with a spicy nut dressing you can't resist that comes together in moments.

SERVES: **2**	YIELD: **3 CUPS**	PREP TIME: **15 MINUTES**	COOK TIME: **10 MINUTES**

SPICY NUT BUTTER DRESSING

¼ cup nut butter

1 inch of fresh ginger root, grated

1 garlic clove, crushed

1 long red chili, deseeded, finely chopped

1 tablespoon tamari

Juice of 1 lime

1 tablespoon pure maple syrup

Half a 14-ounce (400 milliliters) can of coconut milk

THAI QUINOA SALAD

¼ head red cabbage, shredded

8 ounces (250 grams or 1 punnet) cherry tomatoes, halved

1 large carrot, finely sliced or grated

1 cup snow peas, topped and tailed

½ bunch cilantro, chopped

½ bunch basil leaves, chopped

¼ bunch mint leaves, chopped

1 cup quinoa, cooked

Juice of ½ lime

1. In a small bowl, whisk together the nut butter dressing ingredients until combined.

2. In a salad bowl, combine the salad ingredients, drizzle with the spicy dressing, and serve with an extra squeeze of lime.

FM TIP: If you prefer your quinoa warm, add ½ tablespoon of extra virgin olive oil to a frying pan over medium heat and cook the quinoa for 3 to 5 minutes, or until warmed through.

ROASTED CAULIFLOWER SALAD WITH LEMON TAHINI DRESSING

Tahini is a staple ingredient in the Food Matters kitchen because of its versatility, nutty flavor, and nutrient-packed goodness. Here, it really shines in a simple salad dressing but doesn't distract from the hero of the dish, a spiced, roasted cauliflower.

SERVES: 2	YIELD: **3 CUPS**	PREP TIME: **5 MINUTES**	COOK TIME: **25 MINUTES**

1 small head cauliflower, florets cut into bite-size pieces

One 14-ounce (400 grams) can garbanzo beans (chickpeas), drained and rinsed

1 tablespoon extra virgin olive oil

1 teaspoon ground cumin

1 teaspoon sweet smoked paprika

1 ½ teaspoon unrefined sea salt, or to taste, divided

½ teaspoon black pepper, or to taste

1 tablespoon hulled tahini

Juice of 1 lemon

½ tablespoon pure maple syrup

2 cups baby spinach leaves

¼ bunch parsley, chopped

2 Medjool dates, pitted and finely chopped

¼ cup activated almonds, chopped

1 tablespoon hemp seeds

1. Preheat the oven to 350°F (180°C) and line a baking sheet with parchment paper.

2. Place the cauliflower and garbanzo beans on the baking sheet and drizzle with the oil. Sprinkle with the cumin, paprika, salt, and pepper. Roast in the oven for 20 minutes until golden and crispy.

3. While the cauliflower and garbanzo beans are roasting, prepare the dressing by whisking together the tahini, lemon juice, maple syrup, and a pinch of salt and pepper.

4. Combine the cauliflower and garbanzo beans in a large mixing bowl with the spinach, parsley, and dates.

5. Serve topped with the dressing, almonds, and hemp seeds.

FM TIP: For such a simple spice, cumin brings powerful health benefits to the table, including supporting digestion and detoxification, being a rich source of iron, and holding potential cancer-fighting properties.

MAPLE WALNUT HASSELBACK BUTTERNUT SQUASH

This is a staple dish on our Thanksgiving table, because it uses some of the holiday's best seasonal ingredients and is so fun to share. But with a simple side salad, this butternut squash can always be transformed into a meal of its own.

SERVES: 2	YIELD. 2 HALVES	PREP TIME: 15 MINUTES	COOK TIME: 60 MINUTES

1 medium butternut squash (about 2 pounds)

¼ cup pure maple syrup

2 tablespoons extra virgin olive oil

1 tablespoon Dijon mustard

1 tablespoon finely chopped fresh sage leaves, plus garnish

1 teaspoon finely chopped fresh thyme, plus garnish

1 teaspoon unrefined sea salt

½ teaspoon black pepper

4 tablespoons chopped walnuts or pecans

1. Preheat the oven to 350°F (180°C).

2. Cut the butternut squash in half lengthwise, scoop out the seeds and pulp, and discard or save for another recipe.

3. Remove the skin to completely expose the bright orange flesh of the butternut.

4. Place the squash halves cut side down on a roasting pan and bake for 20 minutes, then let slightly cool.

5. While the squash is in the oven, mix the maple syrup, oil, mustard, sage, thyme, salt, and pepper in a small bowl until well combined.

6. Transfer one squash half to a cutting board and place wooden chopsticks or skewers on both sides of the squash to prevent the knife from cutting completely through when you are slicing it.

7. Cut the squash into very thin slices, being careful not to cut the whole way through; you want to leave about ⅓ of an inch joined along the edge. Return the sliced squash to the baking sheet and repeat with the second half.

8. Brush ⅓ of the maple dressing over the squash halves, getting the dressing into the slits of the squash. Set aside 3 tablespoons of dressing for the final steps with the nuts.

(Continued)

9. Place the squash in the oven to bake for 40 to 45 minutes. Baste the squash with the dressing every 10 to 15 minutes; try to avoid removing the entire butternut from the oven while doing this.

10. Add the chopped nuts to the dressing that was set aside, and coat them well. Spoon the dressed nuts over the top of the squash and bake for a final 5 to 8 minutes to brown the nuts.

11. Serve with a sprinkle of fresh herbs and a pinch of salt.

FM TIP: Sage is often overlooked in the spice cabinet or burnt to a fragrant crisp with butter. But this green herb provides more than just flavor. It is actually loaded with beneficial antioxidants, which can support the body throughout life.

ROASTED BUTTERNUT SQUASH & QUINOA SALAD WITH BASIL PESTO

This salad makes for a perfect weeknight dinner, made with just a few staple ingredients, so it comes together in a flash. But as all healthy foodies know, when you can double the recipe it's the ideal recipe to prepare for weekday lunches—just save the sardines till the day of.

SERVES: **2**	YIELD: **3 CUPS**	PREP TIME: **5 MINUTES**	COOK TIME: **20 MINUTES**

½ **butternut squash, peeled, deseeded, and cut into large wedges**

2 beetroots, skin on and cut into wedges

1 tablespoon extra virgin olive oil

1 pinch unrefined sea salt and black pepper

½ **cup quinoa, uncooked**

2 tablespoons Cashew Hemp Basil Pesto (page 208)

One 4-ounce (110 grams) can of sardines in olive oil (or use chickpeas and hemp seeds)

1. Preheat the oven to 350°F (180°C) and line a baking sheet with parchment paper.

2. Place the squash and beets on the baking sheet, drizzle with oil, and season with salt and pepper. Roast in the oven for 20 minutes.

3. Cook the quinoa while the butternut squash and beets are roasting. In a pot, add the quinoa to 1 cup water and bring to a boil. Lower to a simmer, place a lid on the pot, and cook for 15 minutes. Then mix in the Cashew Hemp Basil Pesto.

4. Transfer the quinoa to a bowl, lay the squash and beets on top, and serve with the sardines or optional chickpeas and hemp seeds.

CAULIFLOWER STEAKS
WITH RED PEPPERS & CAPERS

Sides don't always have to be complicated or use a lot of ingredients, and these cauliflower steaks are a testament to that. With the depth of flavor drawn from the antipasto ingredients, it's hard not to make this side the star of the spread.

| SERVES: **2** | YIELD: **4 CAULIFLOWER STEAKS** | PREP TIME: **5 MINUTES** | COOK TIME: **15 MINUTES** |

1 small head cauliflower

1 tablespoon extra virgin olive oil

1 teaspoon unrefined sea salt, or to taste

¼ teaspoon black pepper, or to taste

1 cup green Sicilian olives, chopped

⅓ cup green baby capers, drained

1 red bell pepper, chopped

½ bunch parsley, chopped

Juice of 1 lemon

1 tablespoon activated almonds, roughly chopped

1. Preheat the oven to 350°F (180°C) and line a baking sheet with parchment paper.

2. Slice the cauliflower into 4 even flat slices and place on the baking sheet. Drizzle with the oil and season with salt and pepper, to taste. Roast in the oven for 15 minutes.

3. While the cauliflower is roasting, prepare the salsa. Combine the olives, capers, bell pepper, parsley, lemon juice, and salt and pepper, to taste.

4. Serve the cauliflower with the salsa and a sprinkle of chopped, activated almonds on top.

FM TIP: Capers have been shown to play a role in reducing the severity of arthritis, so whether you have them on your favorite lox bagel or as a standout in this salsa—eat up!

HARISSA SPICED CAULIFLOWER

Harissa is a hot pepper paste from Tunisia that is heavily featured in Middle Eastern, African, and Mediterranean dishes. It has a complex flavor, not too sweet and not too spicy, and it adds a certain something to an otherwise uncomplicated dish.

SERVES: **2**	YIELD: **2 CUPS**	PREP TIME: **5 MINUTES**	COOK TIME: **20 MINUTES**

1 garlic clove, crushed

Juice of ½ lemon

2 tablespoons extra virgin olive oil

1 tablespoon pure maple syrup

1 tablespoon harissa paste

1 head cauliflower, trimmed and cut into florets

2 tablespoons tahini

¼ bunch parsley, roughly chopped

1. Preheat the oven to 350°F (180°C) and line a baking sheet with parchment paper.

2. Combine the garlic, lemon juice, oil, maple syrup, and harissa paste in a large bowl. Add the cauliflower florets and toss to coat well.

3. Spread evenly on the lined baking tray and roast for 20 minutes or until the cauliflower is golden and crisp.

4. Serve drizzled with the tahini and sprinkled with parsley.

JAMES'S GREEN PAPAYA SALAD

In the islands, fresh tropical fruits are in abundance, so we try to use them for breakfast, lunch, and dinner! One of the best ways to enjoy green papaya is in this Thai-inspired salad, where it pairs perfectly with the chili and lime.

SERVES: **2**	YIELD: **3 CUPS**	PREP TIME: **15 MINUTES**	COOK TIME: **NONE**

Juice of 2 limes

2 tablespoons coconut sugar

1 tablespoon tamari

2 garlic cloves, crushed

½ long red chili, deseeded and thinly sliced

1 medium green papaya, peeled, halved, and deseeded

1 medium carrot, peeled

1 handful green beans, topped and thinly sliced

2 spring onions, thinly sliced

1 tomato, diced

½ bunch cilantro, roughly chopped

½ bunch basil, roughly chopped

¼ cup crushed roasted peanuts

1. In a small bowl, whisk the lime juice, coconut sugar, tamari, garlic, and chili until coconut sugar is dissolved. Set aside.

2. Shave or grate the papaya and carrot using a vegetable peeler or box grater into long, thin strands. Place in a large bowl and combine with the green beans, spring onions, tomato, cilantro, and basil.

3. Toss the dressing with the salad and serve with a sprinkle of crushed peanuts.

KALE & SWEET POTATO SALAD WITH ORANGE MISO DRESSING

If there was one dish we could crown king of the superfoods, this would be a leading contender. Bringing together some of the much-loved ingredients in any whole-foods kitchen, with a sweet and zesty hint of citrus popping through, this salad celebrates all things healthy and delicious.

| SERVES: **4** | YIELD: **3 CUPS** | PREP TIME: **10 MINUTES** | COOK TIME: **30 MINUTES** |

POTATO SALAD

1 large sweet potato, peeled and cut into cubes

2 ½ tablespoons extra virgin olive oil, divided

1 tablespoon white miso

½ teaspoon unrefined sea salt, divided

8 to 10 Tuscan kale leaves, removed from stem and torn into bite-size pieces

1 small red onion, thinly sliced

½ bunch parsley, roughly chopped

¼ cup toasted pepitas

1 teaspoon sesame seeds

ORANGE MISO DRESSING

1 tablespoon white miso

2 tablespoons extra virgin olive oil

1 inch of fresh ginger root, grated

Juice of ½ orange

1 to 2 tablespoons warm water

1. Preheat the oven to 350°F (180°C) and line a baking sheet with parchment paper.

2. Toss the sweet potato, 2 tablespoons oil, miso, and ¼ teaspoon salt in a large bowl; coat the sweet potato well.

3. Spread the sweet potato evenly on the lined baking sheet and roast in the oven for 25 to 30 minutes or until the sweet potato begins to brown and is cooked through. Allow to cool slightly.

4. While the sweet potato is cooking, massage ½ tablespoon oil and ¼ teaspoon salt into the kale in a salad bowl. Optionally, you can also steam the kale to help break down the cell wall of the kale leaves, making it easier to digest.

5. Toss the red onion, parsley, and pepitas with the kale. Then toss in the sweet potatoes.

6. Assemble the dressing by whisking together all the dressing ingredients, then drizzle over the salad, tossing to coat.

7. Serve sprinkled with sesame seeds.

FM TIP: Miso is a fermented soy product that has been used for centuries for its medicinal and flavor profiles! It has a slightly nutty, slightly salty, completely umami flavor, making it the star of this dish.

HERBY BROCCOLI TABBOULEH

Typically, tabbouleh is a grain-heavy dish, but we loved it so much that we made a version that's a lot easier to digest, using cruciferous-rich broccoli as the main ingredient. With fresh herbs and an abundance of seasonal veggies, this is the ultimate green dish.

SERVES: **4**	YIELD: **3 CUPS**	PREP TIME: **30 MINUTES**	COOK TIME: **15 MINUTES**

TABBOULEH

2 small heads broccoli, trimmed and cut into florets

1 garlic clove, crushed

1 tablespoon extra virgin olive oil

1 pinch unrefined sea salt and black pepper

1 small Persian or Lebanese cucumber, thinly sliced

½ cup green olives, seeded and halved

½ cup parsley, roughly chopped

½ cup mint, roughly chopped

½ cup basil, roughly chopped

¼ cup toasted pistachios, chopped

CREAMY AVOCADO DRESSING

1 small avocado, halved and seed removed

Zest and juice of 1 lemon

3 tablespoons olive oil

1 tablespoon apple cider vinegar

Pinch of unrefined sea salt

1. Preheat the oven to 350°F (180°C) and line a baking sheet with parchment paper.

2. To make the tabbouleh, pulse the broccoli, garlic, oil, salt, and pepper in a food processor until a "rice" size is formed. Spread the broccoli mixture on the baking tray and bake for 5 to 6 minutes. The baking will lightly cook the raw broccoli, making it easier for you to digest and giving it a nice flavor, but you can skip this step if you like. Allow to cool.

3. In a large salad bowl, toss to combine the broccoli mixture, cucumber, olives, parsley, mint, basil, and pistachios.

4. To make the dressing, you can either blend all the ingredients in a food processor or mix by hand, first mashing the avocado with a fork, then whisking in the other ingredients.

5. Drizzle the dressing over the salad mixture and toss to coat.

FM TIP: Broccoli is often overlooked, but it shouldn't be! This green is a good source of fiber and protein, as well as many essential vitamins and minerals that the body craves.

ASIAN SLAW WITH SESAME TAHINI DRESSING

Sometimes we just need a salad to be simple but still unspeakably delicious. This is when our slaw will become your new must-have. It's delicious and you won't be able to get enough, where the hardest part is slicing your veggies.

| SERVES: **4** | YIELD: **3 CUPS** | PREP TIME: **15 MINUTES** | COOK TIME: **NONE** |

SLAW

1 medium carrot, peeled and finely chopped

½ cup mint, roughly chopped

½ cup cilantro, roughly chopped

2 spring onions, finely chopped

1 pinch unrefined sea salt and black pepper

¼ head purple cabbage, finely shredded

¼ head green cabbage, finely shredded

½ head Napa (wombok) cabbage, finely shredded

SESAME TAHINI DRESSING

1 teaspoon sesame oil

Juice of 1 lemon

1 garlic clove, crushed

2 tablespoons tahini

1 tablespoon rice wine vinegar

1 tablespoon pure maple syrup

3 tablespoons extra virgin olive oil

1. Toss to combine the carrot, mint, cilantro, spring onions, salt, pepper, and purple, green, and Napa cabbages in a large salad bowl.

2. To make the dressing, whisk all the dressing ingredients together in a small bowl until emulsified.

3. Drizzle the salad dressing over the coleslaw and mix well to coat all the ingredients.

FM TIP: It takes a little longer than using a knife, but our tip for getting your cabbage and carrot thinly shredded is to use a julienne or vegetable peeler.

PICKLED MUSHROOM SALAD

Pickling doesn't have to take months of energy for the perfect flavor. Recipes like this salad prove that it can come together in less than half an hour. We love this simple salad as a side for dinner spreads, but you can just as easily enjoy it on its own.

| SERVES: **2 TO 4** | YIELD: **2 CUPS** | PREP TIME: **20 MINUTES** | COOK TIME: **NONE** |

1 garlic clove, crushed

1 inch of fresh ginger root, finely grated

1 long red chili, deseeded and finely sliced

Zest and juice of 2 limes

Zest and juice of 1 lemon

2 cups mixed mushrooms (field, cremini, enoki, shiitake, oyster)

1 pinch unrefined sea salt

½ cup cilantro, roughly chopped

½ cup parsley, roughly chopped

½ cup mint, roughly chopped

1 avocado, halved, deseeded, and cubed

1. Combine the garlic, ginger, chili, lime juice and zest, and lemon juice and zest in a small dish.

2. Clean the mushrooms, removing large stalks, and slice them. The sizing doesn't really matter too much here. We love having a variety of shapes and sizes.

3. In a large salad bowl, pour the citrus dressing over the mushrooms, and add a pinch of salt. Toss to coat the mushrooms and allow them to soften for a few minutes.

4. Add the cilantro, parsley, mint, and avocado. Toss to combine, ensuring all the ingredients are coated in the dressing.

FM TIP: Try to choose whichever mushrooms are in season in your area, including those at your local farmer's market.

MIDDLE EASTERN ROASTED BRUSSELS SPROUTS

Brussels sprouts have unfortunately earned themselves a poor reputation over the years, but most foodies have found a way to make them the star of any table. All it takes is a few deliciously inspired flavors and a little dressing to cut through the crisp, roasted layers.

SERVES: **2 TO 4**	YIELD: **2 CUPS**	PREP TIME: **5 MINUTES**	COOK TIME: **40 MINUTES**

2 cups brussels sprouts, halved lengthwise

1 teaspoon ground cumin

1 teaspoon ground coriander

1 red onion, thinly sliced

1 fennel bulb, thinly sliced

2 tablespoons extra virgin olive oil

½ cup Greek-style or coconut yogurt

1 tablespoon tahini

1 garlic clove, crushed

Zest and juice of 1 lemon

¼ cup hazelnuts, toasted and chopped

1. Preheat the oven to 350°F (180°C) and line a baking sheet with parchment paper.

2. In a bowl, toss the brussel sprouts, cumin, coriander, red onion, fennel, and oil until evenly coated. Spread on the baking sheet.

3. Roast for 35 to 40 minutes or until the brussels sprouts are golden brown and cooked through. Remove them from the oven and allow them to cool slightly.

4. While the brussel sprouts are roasting, assemble the dressing by combining the yogurt, tahini, garlic, and lemon juice and zest.

5. To serve, spread the tahini dressing over a large serving platter, then top with the brussels sprouts and finish with a sprinkle of hazelnuts. Or you can drizzle the dressing over the top.

HONEY HARISSA
ROASTED EGGPLANTS

Eggplant can be one of the more challenging vegetables to cook, but with a foolproof method, you'll never go wrong again. We love it soft and caramelized, and the honey and harissa baste makes this dish sing.

SERVES: 4	YIELD: 8 HALVES	PREP TIME: 5 MINUTES	COOK TIME: 25 MINUTES

3 tablespoons honey

3 tablespoons extra virgin olive oil

½ to 1 tablespoon harissa paste

1 garlic clove, crushed

1 teaspoon ground cumin

1 pinch unrefined sea salt and black pepper

4 small eggplants, halved lengthwise

1. Preheat the oven to 350°F (180°C) and line a baking sheet with parchment paper.

2. Whisk together the honey, oil, harissa paste (1 tablespoon if you like it spicier), garlic, cumin, salt, and pepper in a small bowl.

3. Place the eggplants on the baking sheet, white flesh side facing up, and score a crosshatch pattern on the white flesh.

4. Brush the white flesh of the eggplants with a small amount of the honey harissa dressing and roast the eggplants in the oven for 25 minutes. Every 5 to 10 minutes, brush a little more harissa dressing over the eggplants until used up. Once the eggplants are soft and caramelized, they are ready to serve.

SWEET POTATO, PICKLED ONIONS & SALSA VERDE SALAD

Salsa Verde is a humble hero in our eyes, and with the depth of flavors found in freshly pickled onions alongside freshly roasted sweet potatoes, we can really do no wrong. Enjoy this salad as a side or as a full meal—it's up to you!

SERVES: **4**   YIELD: **2 CUPS**   PREP TIME: **10 MINUTES**   COOK TIME: **40 MINUTES**

Zest and juice of 1 lime

2 tablespoons coconut sugar

3 tablespoons apple cider vinegar

1 teaspoon unrefined sea salt

½ teaspoon freshly ground black pepper

1 large red onion, thinly sliced

2 large sweet potatoes, chopped

2 tablespoons olive oil

1 teaspoon ground cumin

½ cup parsley, roughly chopped

¼ cup toasted pistachios, chopped

3 tablespoons Salsa Verde (page 211)

1. To pickle the onions, mix the lime juice and zest, coconut sugar, apple cider vinegar, salt, and pepper in a large jar or dish until the coconut sugar dissolves. Add the onion to the pickling dressing and allow to sit for at least 2 hours, the longer the better for flavor.

2. Preheat the oven to 350°F (180°C) and line a baking sheet with parchment paper.

3. Spread the sweet potatoes evenly over the baking sheet, drizzle with oil, and sprinkle with cumin. Roast in the oven for 35 to 40 minutes until the sweet potato is cooked through.

4. Serve the sweet potato on a serving platter, topped with the parsley, pistachios, and pickled onions. Drizzle with Salsa Verde.

FM TIP: Not only are pistachios often found in snack bars, but they're one of our favorite sources of fatty acids and potassium and make a crunchy addition to many dishes.

SOUPS &
BROTHS

RESTORATIVE VEGETABLE OR BONE BROTH

A signature recipe of Food Matters, this restorative broth contains minerals for achieving acid-alkaline balance in the body and collagen for skin and cell regeneration. Broths are rich in healing properties to help improve digestion, support the immune system, and enhance the appearance of our skin.

SERVES: **6 TO 8**	YIELD: **8 CUPS**	PREP TIME: **15 MINUTES**	COOK TIME: **10 HOURS**

1 tablespoon extra virgin olive oil

1 large onion, roughly chopped

6 celery stalks, roughly chopped

3 carrots, roughly chopped

4 garlic cloves, crushed

1 bay leaf

1 tablespoon mixed dried Italian herbs (thyme, rosemary, oregano, etc.)

2 tablespoons unrefined sea salt

1 teaspoon black pepper

1 teaspoon ground turmeric

1 inch of fresh ginger root, grated

2 tablespoons apple cider vinegar

1 large chicken or chicken carcass (optional)

1. Add the oil to a large frying pan, pot, or slow cooker pot over medium-high heat, and sauté the onion, celery, carrots, and garlic until they become fragrant and soften.

2. Add the bay leaf, dried herbs, salt, pepper, turmeric, ginger, apple cider vinegar, and 11 cups (2 ¾ quarts) of water.

3. To make vegetable broth, slow cook or simmer the ingredients for 2 to 4 hours on low. To make bone broth, add chicken and slow cook or simmer for 6 to 10 hours on low.

4. Strain the liquid. Allow to cool.

5. Divide the broth into small portions in freezer-safe jars or containers, and store in the fridge if using immediately or in the freezer if using later. The broth can be stored in the fridge for up to one month and in the freezer for 3 to 4 months.

FM TIP: If you are making the Restorative Bone Broth, ensure you choose organic pasture-raised chicken. For an extra-rich flavor, you can roast all the ingredients for 45 to 60 minutes before placing in the slow cooker.

CARAMELIZED CAULIFLOWER & LEEK SOUP

Cauliflower was once considered a fairly boring vegetable that didn't get much attention, but with its high nutritional value and versatility, it deserves a place in the spotlight. This soup showcases just how flavorsome cauliflower can be.

SERVES: **2**	YIELD: **3 CUPS**	PREP TIME: **5 MINUTES**	COOK TIME: **20 MINUTES**

½ **head cauliflower, cut into small florets**

2 **tablespoons extra virgin olive oil, divided**

1 **pinch unrefined sea salt and black pepper, plus more to taste, divided**

1 **yellow onion, finely chopped**

1 **leek, sliced**

1 **cup Restorative Vegetable or Bone Broth (page 272)**

Half a 14-ounce (400 **milliliters) can coconut cream**

¼ **bunch parsley, chopped**

1 **tablespoon activated almonds, roughly chopped**

1. Preheat the oven to 350°F (180°C) and line a baking sheet with parchment paper.

2. Drizzle the cauliflower with 1 tablespoon oil on a baking sheet and season with a pinch of salt and pepper. Roast in the oven for 10 minutes.

3. While the cauliflower is roasting, heat 1 tablespoon oil in a saucepan over medium heat and sauté the onion and leek for 3 to 4 minutes or until caramelized.

4. Add the roasted cauliflower, broth, and coconut cream. Cook for a further 10 minutes.

5. Season with salt and pepper, to taste.

6. Add all the ingredients to a food processor or blender, and blend until smooth.

7. Serve topped with the parsley and almonds.

TOM KHA SOUP
WITH ZUCCHINI NOODLES

If you find yourself missing soul-warming takeout or are looking for a new dish to spice up your weeknights, this Tom Kha Soup is your new go-to meal. With the addition of zucchini noodles and a hearty, rich broth, it's a clear winner.

SERVES: **2**	YIELD: **3 CUPS**	PREP TIME: **15 MINUTES**	COOK TIME: **25 MINUTES**

2 stalks lemongrass

1 tablespoon coconut oil

1 yellow onion, diced

2 garlic cloves, minced

2 inches of fresh ginger root, peeled and thinly sliced

1 long red chili, deseeded and thinly sliced

½ cup Restorative Vegetable or Bone Broth (page 272)

One 14-ounce (400 milliliters) can coconut cream

1 cup white mushrooms, sliced

1 tomato, cubed

Juice of 1 lime

1 tablespoon tamari

½ tablespoon pure maple syrup

2 medium zucchini, spiralized

¼ lime

½ cup cilantro (coriander), chopped

1. To prepare the lemongrass, slice off the thick ends of the stalks. Then, using the back of your knife, lightly bang the stalks to release the oils. Next, slice the stalks into smaller strips.

2. Cook the coconut oil and lemongrass stalks in a large pot over medium-high heat for 1 to 2 minutes or until the lemongrass is fragrant. Add the onion and sauté until the onion begins to soften.

3. Reduce heat to medium and add the garlic, ginger, and chili, cooking for another minute until fragrant.

4. Add the broth and coconut cream and bring to a boil. Reduce the heat and continue to simmer for 10 to 15 minutes. Using a slotted spoon, remove the lemongrass from the soup and discard.

5. Stir in the mushrooms, tomato, lime juice, tamari, and maple syrup and continue to simmer for another 5 to 8 minutes.

6. Ladle the soup on top of the zucchini. Serve topped with a squeeze of lime and cilantro.

MEXICAN SOUP

Give your mouth the fiesta it deserves with this hearty Mexican-spiced tomato soup!

SERVES: **2**	YIELD: **4 CUPS**	PREP TIME: **15 MINUTES**	COOK TIME: **20 MINUTES**

3 tablespoons extra virgin olive oil, divided

2 large red bell peppers, chopped

4 large vine-ripened tomatoes, halved

½ teaspoon unrefined sea salt, or to taste

¼ teaspoon black pepper, or to taste

1 small yellow onion, diced

2 garlic cloves, crushed

2 cups Restorative Vegetable Broth (page 272)

1 teaspoon ground cumin

2 teaspoons ground paprika

½ teaspoon chili powder

½ avocado, diced

Juice of 1 lime

¼ cup cilantro, chopped

1 cup Rosemary & Sea Salt Cassava Crackers (optional, page 327)

1. Preheat the oven to 350°F (180°C).

2. Drizzle 2 tablespoons oil over the peppers and tomatoes on a baking tray, and sprinkle with salt and pepper. Bake for 30 to 40 minutes until very soft. Allow to cool.

3. Heat a saucepan over medium-high heat, add the remaining tablespoon of oil, and sauté the onion for 2 to 3 minutes or until golden brown and softened. Add the garlic and sauté for 2 to 3 minutes or until fragrant.

4. Add the roasted peppers and tomatoes, broth, cumin, paprika, and chili powder. Simmer for 10 to 15 minutes.

5. Allow the soup to slightly cool. In a blender or food processor, blend in batches until you have a smooth puree. Taste and add salt and pepper, as needed.

6. Top with the avocado, lime, and cilantro and serve with some crunchy Rosemary & Sea Salt Cassava Crackers.

CREAMY AYURVEDIC BUTTERNUT SOUP

This smooth, warming soup is perfect for those chilly winter days and packed with Ayurvedic spices to support the digestive and immune systems.

SERVES: **2**	YIELD: **4 CUPS**	PREP TIME: **15 MINUTES**	COOK TIME: **20 MINUTES**

1 butternut squash, peeled and cubed (yields about 3 cups cooked)

4 tablespoons coconut oil, divided

1 tablespoon medium curry powder

1 yellow onion, diced

2 garlic cloves, crushed

2 inches of fresh ginger root, grated

½ teaspoon unrefined sea salt, or to taste

¼ teaspoon black pepper, or to taste

2 teaspoons ground turmeric

½ cup nut butter

2 cups Restorative Vegetable or Bone Broth (page 272)

One 14-ounce (400 milliliters) can coconut milk

Cilantro, lime, and/or toasted gluten-free bread (optional)

1. Preheat the oven to 350°F (180°C). Coat the butternut squash in 3 tablespoons coconut oil and roast for 30 to 40 minutes or until golden brown and soft.

2. Heat a large pot over medium heat, add the curry powder, and dry toast for 1 minute.

3. Add the remaining tablespoon coconut oil, then add the onion, garlic, and ginger, and sauté for 2 minutes.

4. Season with salt and pepper.

5. Add the butternut squash, turmeric, nut butter, broth, and coconut milk to the saucepan, stir well, and simmer for 15 to 20 minutes.

6. Allow the soup to slightly cool, then blend in batches in a blender or food processor until you have a smooth puree. Add salt and pepper as needed. You can serve topped with cilantro, lime, toasted gluten-free bread, or whatever you prefer.

DESSERTS & SWEET TREATS

HAZELNUT TRUFFLES

These truffles are easy to make and oh so delicious. You may want to double the ingredients and make a double batch because they sure don't last long in the Food Matters headquarters!

SERVES: **16**   YIELD: **16 TRUFFLES**   PREP TIME: **20 MINUTES**   COOK TIME: **NONE**

½ cup (80 grams) vegan chocolate chips (at least 85 percent dark), roughly chopped

½ cup coconut milk

1 pinch unrefined sea salt

¼ cup pure maple syrup

¾ cup almond, ABC, or cashew butter

1 teaspoon hazelnut extract or vanilla extract

1 cup roasted hazelnuts

1. Boil a small pot of water and place a glass bowl containing the chocolate over the hot water bath. Once the chocolate has melted, remove the pot from the heat but keep the bowl over the hot water.

2. While you melt the chocolate, gently warm the coconut milk in a small pot over low heat. Add a generous pinch of salt.

3. Slowly add the warm coconut milk to the melted chocolate while continuously whisking over low heat.

4. Whisk in the maple syrup, nut butter, and hazelnut extract.

5. Allow the mixture to cool, then refrigerate it overnight to harden.

6. Before taking the mixture out of the fridge, put aside at least 20 whole hazelnuts and chop the rest finely. Spread the chopped hazelnuts on a tray.

7. Scoop about 1 tablespoon of the ganache mixture and roll into a ball. Flatten the balls into the palm of your hand, place a hazelnut in the middle, and then close the truffle mixture around the hazelnut and roll it back into a ball. Don't worry if these aren't perfect in size.

8. Roll the truffle between the palms of your hands and then roll it in the chopped hazelnuts. Continue until all the mixture is gone. Store in the fridge for up to one month.

LEMON CURD TARTS

It's no secret that we love lemons here at Food Matters. Lemon water in the mornings, lemon curd tarts for dessert . . . It's all about balance.

| SERVES: **6 TO 8** | YIELD: **6 SMALL TARTS** | PREP TIME: **20 MINUTES** | SETTING TIME: **60 MINUTES** |

2 teaspoons coconut oil

1 tablespoon shredded coconut

TART BASE

½ cup macadamia nuts

½ cup gluten-free oats

¼ cup almonds

1 cup pitted Medjool dates

3 teaspoons rice malt syrup

1 pinch unrefined sea salt

LEMON CURD

3 organic free-range eggs

Zest of 2 lemons

¼ cup honey

½ cup freshly squeezed lemon juice

4 tablespoons coconut oil

1 teaspoon vanilla extract

1 tablespoon cacao butter (optional)

1. Grease the bottom and sides of a tart pan with the coconut oil and sprinkle a little shredded coconut over the springform to prevent the tart from sticking. In a food processor or high-speed blender, pulse all the tart base ingredients until well combined.

2. Cover the base and sides of the tart pan with the dough and press down firmly. Freeze to set for around 20 minutes.

3. To make the lemon curd, whisk together the eggs, lemon zest, and honey in a saucepan on low heat. Add the lemon juice, coconut oil, vanilla extract, and cacao butter, if using, and continue to whisk on medium heat until everything is melted and the mixture starts to thicken. If it's taking a while to thicken, take away from the heat for a couple of minutes, then return to the heat and continue to lightly whisk until bubbles start to appear and a creamy consistency has formed.

4. Pour the curd into your prepared tart pan, covering the base as evenly as possible. Refrigerate for 40 to 60 minutes to set.

FM TIP: Despite being acidic in taste, lemons are actually alkaline in nature! This means they can support in correcting acidity imbalances in the body.

NO-BAKE CHOC-CARAMEL PEANUT BARS

Imagine the peanutty goodness of a Snickers bar, the mouthwatering sweetness of a Caramello, and the health benefits of using natural, whole foods. If you can't quite imagine it, with this recipe, you can taste it!

| SERVES: **10 TO 12** | YIELD: **10 TO 12 BARS** | PREP TIME: **20 MINUTES** | SETTING TIME: **60 MINUTES** |

1 packed cup Medjool dates, pitted and halved

2 tablespoons peanut butter or other nut butter

1 teaspoon vanilla extract

1 teaspoon maca powder

¼ teaspoon unrefined sea salt

⅔ cup oat flour

½ cup peanuts, roughly chopped

1 cup vegan chocolate chips (at least 85 percent dark)

1. Cover the dates with ½ cup boiling water, or enough to submerge them in a bowl, for 5 minutes. This helps to make the dates softer, which allows you to create the most amazing caramel. Drain the liquid and add the dates to the food processor.

2. Add the peanut butter, vanilla extract, maca powder, and salt to the food processor and process until a sticky caramel sauce is formed. Scrape down the sides as needed. Remove the caramel mixture from the food processor and set aside.

3. Without cleaning the food processor, process the oat flour with ¼ cup of the caramel mixture until mixed well.

4. Press the oat mixture into a small rectangular lined dish or silicone mold firmly and evenly.

5. Cover the oat mixture with the remaining caramel mixture, spreading evenly. Sprinkle the caramel layer with the peanuts, pressing lightly into the caramel. Freeze for 1 to 2 hours to set.

6. Once the mixture is firmly set, carefully remove it from the mold.

7. Slice into 10 to 12 thin bars and place back in the freezer while you prepare the chocolate.

(Continued)

8. Using the double-boiler method (see Step 1 of Hazelnut Truffles, page 284), completely melt the chocolate. Remove the bars from the freezer. You will need to do the next step fairly quickly.

9. Using two forks, dip each bar into the melted chocolate and flip to coat both sides.

10. Place on a lined plate with parchment paper and repeat until all bars are done. Set in the fridge for 10 to 15 minutes.

FM TIP: It's best to make these bars in a silicone mold that is flexible enough for easy removal. Alternatively, line a small glass rectangular dish with parchment paper for easy removal.

COCONUT RASPBERRY CHIA BARS

This is a fresh take on the delicious coconut and raspberry cookies we grew up loving. With a crumbly coconut crust and a delicious jelly filling that can only be made with chia, you'll have to share this one.

| SERVES. **8 TO 10** | YIELD: **8 TO 10 SLICES** | PREP TIME: **15 MINUTES** | COOKING TIME: **30 MINUTES** |

RASPBERRY CHIA SEED JAM

2 cups raspberries, fresh or frozen

1 tablespoon pure maple syrup

¼ cup chia seeds

Juice of 1 lemon

COCONUT BASE

½ cup coconut oil, melted

⅓ cup pure maple syrup

1½ cups almond meal

2 cups shredded coconut

1 organic free-range egg

COCONUT CRUMBLE

2 organic free-range eggs

2 cups shredded coconut

1. Preheat the oven to 355° F (180° C) and line a square baking pan with parchment paper.

2. To make the raspberry chia seed jam, stir the raspberries in a small saucepan over medium heat until the fruit softens, breaks down, and gently simmers. Mash the raspberries with a fork or vegetable masher. Stir in the maple syrup, chia seeds, and lemon juice. Combine well and remove from heat. Allow it to cool so the jam can thicken.

3. To make the coconut base, combine the coconut oil, maple syrup, almond meal, coconut, and egg in a bowl. Mix well and press firmly into the square pan, spreading evenly with the back of a spoon. Bake for 10 to 15 minutes or until firm to the touch and golden around the edges. Allow to slightly cool, but leave oven on.

4. To make the coconut crumble, whisk the eggs in a bowl until frothy, then whisk in the coconut.

5. Spread the jam evenly over the baked coconut base, then top with the coconut crumble, pressing down lightly. Bake for another 10 to 15 minutes or until the coconut mixture on top is set and golden brown.

6. Allow to cool before removing from the pan and slicing into bars.

SWEET POTATO BROWNIE WITH CHOC-AVO FROSTING

If there's one thing we know how to do, it's hiding delicious fruits and vegetables in unassuming places. These sweet potato brownies are delectably gooey, and the inclusion of avocado in the frosting adds an extra layer of creamy goodness to every bite.

SERVES: **8 TO 10**	YIELD: **8 TO 10 SLICES**	PREP TIME: **15 MINUTES**	COOKING TIME: **35 MINUTES**

SWEET POTATO BROWNIE

1 medium sweet potato, peeled and cubed (or 1 cup sweet potato puree)

½ cup pure maple syrup

½ cup nut butter

1 teaspoon vanilla extract

2 tablespoons coconut oil, melted

½ cup raw cacao powder

½ teaspoon unrefined sea salt

1 teaspoon baking powder

1 cup oat flour

CHOC-AVO FROSTING

1 avocado, halved and deseeded

¼ cup raw cacao powder

3 tablespoon pure maple syrup

1. Preheat the oven to 350° F (180° C) and line a square baking pan with parchment paper.

2. To make the sweet potato brownie, bring a large pot of water to boil, and cook the sweet potato until it is soft enough to poke with a fork. Drain, allow to cool, and mash or whisk until a smooth puree is formed. You could also add the cooked sweet potato to a food processor and process it until smooth.

3. Transfer 1 cup of the sweet potato puree to a large mixing bowl. Add the maple syrup, nut butter, vanilla extract, and coconut oil and combine well.

4. Add the cacao powder, salt, baking powder, and oat flour and mix until well combined.

5. Pour the sweet potato batter into the lined pan and spread evenly. Bake for 30 to 35 minutes or until the brownie is firm to the touch or an inserted skewer comes out clean. Allow to cool.

6. To make the frosting, whisk the avocado, cacao powder, and maple syrup in a bowl until smooth. Adjust the sweetness with a little more maple syrup if you prefer.

7. Once the brownie is cooled, remove it from the pan and evenly cover it with the frosting. Slice into squares to serve.

STORAGE TIP: These brownies keep well in the freezer without the frosting—just make sure to slice before freezing. Defrost as needed and top with Choc-Avo Frosting before serving.

FM TIP: Most stores will carry hulled or unhulled tahini, which is essentially sesame seed butter. Hulled means that the outer layer of "skin" has been removed from the seed before processing, and it's more subtle in flavor and has a creamier texture than unhulled tahini.

SALTED CARAMEL & MACADAMIA BLONDIE

Blondies are the angelic alternative to sinful brownies, and these salted caramel and macadamia-based treats are no exception. We use tahini as a nourishing base for these blondies, but you'll never know it's there!

SERVES: 8 TO 10	YIELD: 8 TO 10 SLICES	PREP TIME: 15 MINUTES	COOKING TIME: 35 MINUTES

SALTED CARAMEL

¼ cup (2 ounces) canned coconut cream

¼ cup coconut sugar

½ teaspoon unrefined sea salt

1 teaspoon coconut oil

1 teaspoon vanilla extract

BLONDIE

4 tablespoons coconut oil, melted

¼ cup pure maple syrup

1 teaspoon vanilla extract

¼ cup (2 ounces) canned coconut cream

1 cup tahini

½ cup oat flour

1 teaspoon baking powder

½ teaspoon unrefined sea salt

½ cup macadamia nuts, roughly chopped

1. Preheat the oven to 350° F (180° C) and line a square baking pan with parchment paper.

2. To make the salted caramel sauce, add the coconut cream, coconut sugar, and salt to a small pot over medium heat. Bring to a boil and reduce the heat as soon as it starts to boil (make sure you keep a close eye on this). Stir in the coconut oil and vanilla extract, and continue stirring until the sauce begins to thicken, about 10 to 15 minutes. Allow it to slightly cool, then transfer it to a glass jar.

3. To make the blondie, whisk to combine the coconut oil, maple syrup, vanilla extract, coconut cream, ¼ cup room temperature water, and tahini in a large bowl.

4. Fold in the oat flour, baking powder, salt, and macadamia nuts, mixing well.

5. Spread the blondie batter evenly into the prepared baking pan. Dollop teaspoons of the salted caramel sauce on top of the batter. Use a skewer or knife to swirl the caramel sauce through the mixture. (This doesn't need to look perfect.)

6. Bake for 30 to 35 minutes or until the blondie is firm to the touch or an inserted skewer comes out clean. Allow it to cool.

7. Remove the blondies from the pan and slice into squares. Drizzle with extra salted caramel sauce if you have any left over.

NO-BAKE CHOCOLATE ORANGE TART

There's something about chocolate and orange that will always be a winning combination in our eyes. There's a hint of intensity with the citrus, nurtured by a creamy chocolate flavor that we all know and love. So of course we've put a uniquely Food Matters spin on this tasty tart.

SERVES: **8 TO 10**   YIELD: **8 TO 10 SLICES**   PREP TIME: **15 MINUTES**   SETTING TIME: **60 MINUTES**

TART BASE

½ cup shredded coconut

1 cup mixed seeds (pepitas, sunflower, sesame)

1 cup Medjool dates

4 tablespoons coconut oil

CHOCOLATE ORANGE LAYER

2 avocados, halved and deseeded

¼ cup coconut oil

1 teaspoon vanilla extract

Zest of 1 orange

½ cup raw cacao powder

1. To make the tart base, grind the coconut, seeds, dates, and coconut oil in a food processor or high-speed blender until a sticky crumble forms. Press the mixture in a 9-inch (20 centimeters) fluted cake pan (or any rectangular dish, 7-inch springform cake pan). Smooth with the back of a spoon and set in the freezer while you make your chocolate layer.

2. To make the chocolate layer, process all the chocolate layer ingredients in a food processor or high-speed blender until smooth and creamy.

3. Spread the chocolate layer evenly over the tart base and freeze for 1 hour to set.

4. Remove from the freezer 5 to 10 minutes before serving.

   FM TIP: If you want to use individual tart tins to help ration the portions to eat throughout the week, you can do that too! The recipe still stays the same; just divide the dough among the individual tarts.

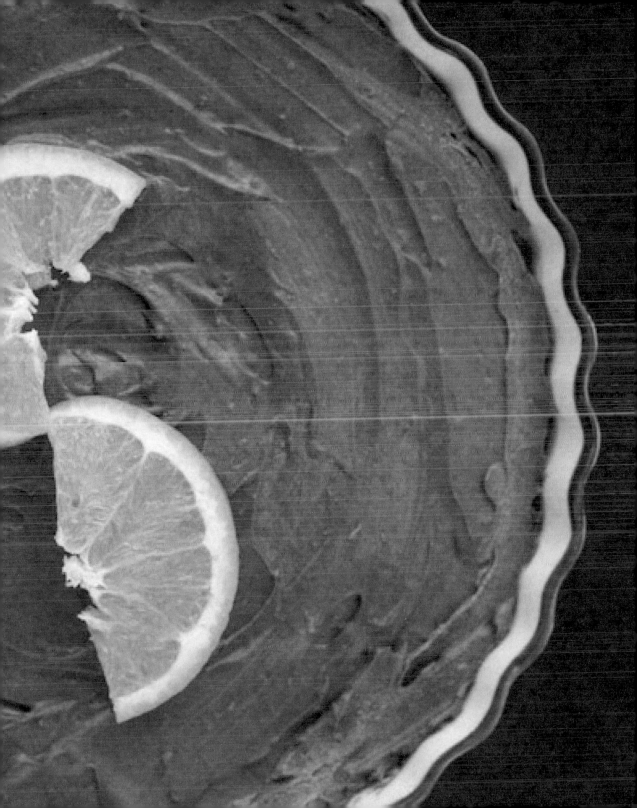

MACADAMIA & COCONUT PEACH CRUMBLE WITH DAIRY-FREE VANILLA ICE CREAM

MACADAMIA & COCONUT PEACH CRUMBLE

Crumble is one of those desserts that's always nourishing for the mind, body, and soul. But living next to the beach, we're not often craving a hot treat! That's why macadamia and coconut, with the firm, ripe seasonal peaches, give us the taste of summer that we enjoy year-round.

SERVES: **8**	YIELD: **4 CUPS**	PREP TIME: **20 MINUTES**	COOKING TIME: **15 MINUTES**

6 ripe peaches, pitted and roughly chopped

2 tablespoons coconut sugar

Juice of 1 lemon

1 teaspoon vanilla extract

1 cup rolled oats

1 cup shredded coconut

¼ cup macadamia nuts, roughly chopped

½ cup nut butter

2 tablespoons pure maple syrup

1 teaspoon ground cinnamon

1. Preheat the oven to 350° F (180° C).

2. Add the peaches, coconut sugar, lemon juice, and vanilla extract in a large saucepan or oven-safe frying pan over medium heat. Simmer, stirring continuously, until the peaches soften and the coconut sugar dissolves and begins to caramelize.

3. Pour the peach filling into a baking dish if you wish, or leave the filling in the ovenproof frying pan.

4. In a bowl, combine the oats, coconut, macadamia nuts, nut butter, maple syrup, and cinnamon.

5. Evenly spread the oat crumble over the peach filling, pressing down lightly. Bake for 15 minutes or until the crumble is golden brown.

6. Serve topped with Dairy-Free Vanilla Ice Cream (page 301).

FM TIP: If fresh peaches aren't available, you can adapt this recipe with other juicy, nutrient-rich stone fruit—nectarines, plums, apricots, or even mixed berries. It may be more or less tart, but the nourishing health benefits remain the same.

DAIRY-FREE
VANILLA ICE CREAM

Ice cream is one of those classics that always tastes so much better when you've made it fresh. We've swapped out traditional dairy for an island favorite, coconut cream, to truly bring out that tropical vanilla flavor.

SERVES: **8**	YIELD: **2 PINTS**	PREP TIME: **10 MINUTES**	SETTING TIME: **45 MINUTES WITH ICE CREAM MAKER, UP TO 6 HOURS WITH FREEZER METHOD**

Two 14-ounce (400 grams) cans coconut cream

½ cup pure maple syrup

1 pinch unrefined sea salt

1 vanilla bean, seeds scraped out

2 teaspoons vanilla extract

1. Mix all the ingredients in a small bowl and combine well.

2. If you are using an ice cream maker, pour the mixture into the ice cream maker and churn for approximately 45 minutes or according to your machine's instructions. Once finished, transfer to a freezer-safe container, cover, and freeze for at least 5 hours.

3. If you don't have an ice cream maker, freeze the mixed mixture in a freezer-safe container. Every hour, remove the mixture from the freezer and whisk it to infuse air into the mixture. Repeat for 5 to 6 hours. Then freeze until completely frozen. The result won't be as creamy, but it is still a delightful frozen treat.

FM TIP: Our dairy-free ice cream is made with coconut cream rather than dairy. While coconut cream is considered a saturated fat, much of it consists of lauric acid—which is essential in supporting a strong, healthy immune system.

NUT BUTTER FUDGE

For this recipe, let your creativity and nut butter collections run wild. The fudge recipe itself is so simple, you can try it with any nut butter to get a feel for your favorite.

SERVES. **10**   YIELD: **10 SLICES**   PREP TIME: **5 MINUTES**   SETTING TIME: **30 MINUTES**

½ cup raw cacao powder

¼ cup pure maple syrup

½ cup coconut oil, melted

1 teaspoon vanilla extract

¼ cup nut butter (cashew, peanut, almond, Brazil)

¼ cup fresh or frozen raspberries

3 tablespoons activated buckwheat groats, quinoa puffs, rolled oats, or chopped nuts

1. Whisk the cacao, maple syrup, coconut oil, and vanilla extract in a medium mixing bowl until well combined.

2. Add the nut butter and combine.

3. Mix in the raspberries and buckwheat groats/quinoa puffs.

4. Pour the mixture into a lined tray or freezer-safe container.

5. Freeze for 30 minutes or until set.

6. Cut or break into pieces to enjoy.

KIDS' FAVORITES

MINI CASSAVA BANANA PANCAKES WITH CHOCOLATE CHIPS

Nothing says Sunday morning breakfast with the family quite like a stack of pancakes. The added bonus of our favorite pancake recipe is that they're packed with nourishing ingredients, and little chefs love to help make them!

SERVES: **4**   YIELD: **15 TO 20 MINI PANCAKES**   PREP TIME: **10 MINUTES**   COOK TIME: **10 MINUTES**

2 organic free-range eggs

2 ripe bananas, mashed

1 teaspoon vanilla extract

½ cup cassava flour

½ teaspoon baking soda

½ cup unsweetened plant-based milk of choice (coconut, almond, oat)

¼ cup dairy-free chocolate chips

Coconut oil for cooking

½ cup frozen mixed berries, thawed

¼ cup coconut yogurt

¼ cup tablespoon nut butter

1. Whisk the eggs, bananas, and vanilla extract in a bowl to begin forming a batter.

2. Fold in the cassava flour and baking soda, then gradually add the plant-based milk. You don't want the batter to be too runny. Add a little more plant-based milk or water if you need to thin out the mixture.

3. Fold in the chocolate chips and mix well.

4. Heat 1 tablespoon of coconut oil in a medium frying pan and pour in 2 tablespoons of the mixture to make a mini pancake. Let the pancake cook for 1 to 2 minutes or until bubbles begin to form. Flip and let the other side cook for another 1 to 2 minutes. Repeat, oiling the pan as needed.

5. After you have cooked all the batter, in the same frying pan over medium heat, add the mixed berries and mash until a jam-like consistency is achieved.

6. Serve the pancakes topped with the mixed berries, a dollop of coconut yogurt, and nut butter.

NOTE: This is a version of our cassava pancakes and our famous 2-Ingredient Pancakes (page 105). We wanted to create something for the kids that had bananas along with a nice dose of fiber from the cassava flour!

4 WAYS TO USE THIS SAUCE

1. Pizza-base sauce in our Mini Lunch-Box Pizzas (page 317)
2. Pasta sauce for our Sweet Potato Gnocchi (page 164)
3. As the base sauce in our Spinach & Harissa Shakshuka (page 122)
4. Dipping sauce for Crunchy Cauliflower Nuggets (page 313)

THE HIDDEN VEGETABLE PASTA SAUCE

If only it was as easy to get kids to eat vegetables as it is pasta! That's exactly why The Hidden Vegetable Pasta Sauce is a household favorite—it's nutrient-packed, incredibly versatile, and more delicious than versions from the grocer!

SERVES: **10**	YIELD: **8 CUPS**	PREP TIME: **20 MINUTES**	COOK TIME: **30 MINUTES**

1 tablespoon extra virgin olive oil

1 yellow onion, finely diced

2 garlic cloves, crushed

3 celery stalks, finely diced

2 medium zucchini, finely diced

1 red bell pepper, finely diced

2 carrots, finely diced

2 cups baby spinach, roughly chopped

½ teaspoon dried oregano

½ teaspoon dried thyme

½ teaspoon dried basil

1 teaspoon sweet smoked paprika

1 bottle (700 grams, 24 ounces, 3 cups) organic passata sauce

2 cups Restorative Vegetable or Bone Broth (page 272)

1 tablespoon tomato paste

½ bunch fresh basil leaves

1. Add the oil, onion, and garlic in a large pot over medium heat. Cook for 2 to 3 minutes or until the onion becomes translucent.

2. Add the celery, zucchini, bell pepper, carrots, and spinach and cook for around 15 minutes, continually stirring until the vegetables soften. Add the oregano, thyme, basil, and paprika and stir for 1 minute.

3. Add the passata, vegetable broth, and tomato paste. Stir to combine well. Bring to a boil, then reduce the heat and simmer for 15 minutes.

4. Allow the sauce to slightly cool, then add the fresh basil leaves and blend to a smooth consistency.

5. Allow the sauce to fully cool. Serve, refrigerate, or freeze in portion sizes.

TIPS FOR STORING: This makes a lot of sauce. We love keeping some in the fridge to use throughout the week, then freezing the remaining sauce into portions to use for different recipes. Freeze in freezer-safe containers or ice cube trays for quick use.

HEALTHY MAC 'N' CHEESE WITH HIDDEN VEGGIES

If there's one dish that keeps kids coming back for more, it's mac 'n' cheese. This healthified version brings the same delicious, creamy flavors that we all know and love to the table, all while being almost entirely veggie-based.

| SERVES: **4** | YIELD: **3 CUPS** | PREP TIME: **15 MINUTES** | COOK TIME: **30 MINUTES** |

1 packet (12 ounces) gluten-free macaroni pasta (quinoa or brown rice)

½ cup raw cashews, soaked overnight in filtered water

2 carrots, peeled and chopped into cubes

½ butternut squash, peeled and chopped into cubes

½ head cauliflower, cut into florets

1 teaspoon sweet smoked paprika

½ teaspoon ground turmeric

1 garlic clove, crushed

⅓ cup nutritional yeast

Juice of ½ lemon

1 teaspoon apple cider vinegar

½ to 1 cup Restorative Vegetable or Bone Broth (page 272)

1 teaspoon unrefined sea salt

2 tablespoons extra virgin olive oil

Brazil Nut Parmesan (optional, page 215)

1. Bring a large pot of salted water to a boil. Add the pasta and cook according to package instructions or until al dente. Drain and set aside.

2. Drain and rinse the soaked cashews.

3. Steam the carrots, butternut squash, and cauliflower in a vegetable steamer for 7 to 8 minutes or until the vegetables are tender.

4. Blend the steamed vegetables, cashews, paprika, turmeric, garlic, nutritional yeast, lemon juice, apple cider vinegar, ½ cup vegetable broth, salt, and oil in a blender or food processor until smooth. Add more vegetable broth if you need it.

5. Add the vegetable mixture to the pot with the pasta and mix well to coat the pasta. You can do this over low heat for 4 to 5 minutes to warm the sauce through, continually stirring.

6. Serve with a sprinkle of the Brazil Nut Parmesan for extra crunch and flavor.

FM TIP: Steaming foods, rather than boiling them, helps to retain their nutritional value. When vegetables are boiled, many of the good nutrients can leach into the water and get tipped down the drain. Steaming is not much more difficult or time-consuming, and it helps to preserve the incredible vitamins and minerals these foods have to offer.

CRUNCHY CAULIFLOWER NUGGETS

These nuggets are loved by kids and adults alike—mainly because the flavors take you back to a fast-food favorite in just one bite. The extra serving of veggies is just an added bonus! Plus, by baking instead of frying, we're making them even healthier (and just as crispy).

SERVES: **4**	YIELD: **3 CUPS**	PREP TIME: **15 MINUTES**	COOK TIME: **30 MINUTES**

1 cup almond meal

1 teaspoon sweet smoked paprika

1 teaspoon ground cumin

1 teaspoon ground turmeric

1 cup unsweetened plant-based milk of choice (coconut, almond, oat)

½ cup oat flour or gluten-free flour

½ head cauliflower, cut into bite-sized florets

Unrefined sea salt and black pepper to taste

1. Preheat the oven to 350°F (180°C) and line a baking tray with parchment paper.

2. Combine the almond meal, paprika, cumin, and turmeric in a medium bowl to make a crumbly mixture.

3. Mix the plant-based milk and oat flour in another bowl to make the batter. Mix well.

4. Coat the cauliflower florets in the flour batter, a few at a time, then toss in the almond meal spice mix, coating well.

5. Place the cauliflower on the lined baking tray and bake for 25 to 30 minutes or until golden brown.

FM TIP: Cauliflower is a great source of the essential nutrient choline. This nutrient supports the learning and memory centers of the brain.

CHOCOLATE BANANA POPS

Summer days for us always included ice cream by the beach. These Chocolate Banana Pops are the perfect alternative for healthy kids on sunny days!

SERVES: **12**   YIELD: **12 POPS**   PREP TIME: **15 MINUTES**   COOK TIME: **30 MINUTES**

6 ripe bananas, peeled and halved

1 cup dairy-free chocolate chips

3 tablespoons coconut oil

OPTIONAL TOPPINGS

Toasted coconut

Chopped nuts

Sea salt flakes

Crushed chocolate

TOOLS

12 popsicle sticks

1. Line a baking tray with parchment paper.

2. Insert a popsicle stick into the cut side of each banana half and place the bananas on the lined baking tray. Freeze for 4 to 5 hours or overnight.

3. Lay out all of your chosen toppings on separate plates before you take the bananas out of the freezer. You will need to work fast.

4. In a small saucepan over medium-low heat, combine the chocolate chips and coconut oil, continuously stirring until smooth and completely melted.

5. Transfer the melted chocolate to a tall glass or bowl for easy dipping. Dip each frozen banana piece into the chocolate mixture, then place back onto the parchment paper and immediately coat in toppings. Repeat with the remaining bananas and place back in the freezer to set.

6. Store in an airtight, freezer-safe container for up to 2 months.

STORAGE TIP: If taking your banana pops to the beach, make sure they're kept cool! The chocolate can melt quickly on hot days.

MINI LUNCH-BOX PIZZAS

These lunch-box pizzas are an easy staple for nutritious meal prep throughout the week, but here's a secret—kids love to have them at birthday parties too! They're so simple and bound to become a new family favorite.

SERVES: **4**   YIELD: **10 TO 12 MINI PIZZAS**   PREP TIME: **10 MINUTES**   COOK TIME: **12 MINUTES**

4 Homemade Gluten-Free wraps (page 220) or tortillas

1 cup Hidden Vegetable Pasta Sauce (page 309)

½ cup spinach, shredded

½ cup basil, shredded

1 small red bell pepper, thinly sliced

1 small carrot, grated

1 cup grated organic cheese

1. Preheat the oven to 350°F (180°C). Lightly oil a 12-cup muffin tin.

2. Lay the tortillas on a flat surface and, using a can or cookie cutter, cut 3 to 4 medium circles into each one, pressing firmly enough in a rocking motion to cut through the tortillas.

3. Fit a tortilla circle into each of the muffin tins, pressing carefully to make sure the center is kept open.

4. Scoop a little sauce onto each tortilla. Top with the spinach, basil, bell pepper, carrot, and grated cheese.

5. Bake for 10 to 12 minutes, or until cheese has melted.

ONE-BOWL GLUTEN-FREE CHOCOLATE CAKE

It can be hard to get baking right with little hands at play. This simple cake is one you'll want to get the whole family involved with! There's minimal equipment needed, just a whole lot of mixing—which is always better when taken in turns.

SERVES: **8 TO 10**   YIELD: **10 SLICES**   PREP TIME: **20 MINUTES**   COOK TIME: **35 MINUTES**

CAKE

1 cup plus 1½ teaspoons cacao powder, divided

2 ripe bananas, mashed

¼ cup unsweetened applesauce

1 teaspoon vanilla extract

½ cup pure maple syrup

2 tablespoons nut butter

2 teaspoon baking soda

1¼ cups unsweetened plant-based milk of choice (coconut, almond, oat)

2 cups gluten-free all-purpose flour

CHOCOLATE FROSTING

½ cup almond, ABC, or cashew butter

4 tablespoon pure maple syrup

¼ cup raw cacao powder

4 tablespoons unsweetened plant-based milk of choice (coconut, almond, oat)

1 teaspoon vanilla extract

1. Preheat the oven to 350°F (180°C). Line an 8-inch round cake pan with parchment paper or grease with coconut oil, dust with 1 ½ teaspoons cacao powder, then shake excess loose and discard.

2. Add the mashed banana, applesauce, vanilla extract, maple syrup, nut butter, baking soda, and plant-based milk in a large mixing bowl, whisking to combine.

3. Sift in the gluten-free flour and 1 cup cacao powder, whisking to combine. You don't want the consistency of the batter to be too thick, but also not too watery. If it's too thick, add a little more plant-based milk; if it's too runny, add a little more gluten-free flour.

4. Pour the batter into the prepared cake tin and bake for 30 to 35 minutes, or until an inserted skewer comes out clean.

5. Allow to cool in the cake pan for around 15 minutes before removing and placing on a cooling rack.

6. To make the chocolate frosting, mix the nut butter, maple syrup, cacao powder, plant-based milk, and vanilla extract in a medium bowl until well combined. You may want to add in 1 to 2 tablespoons of hot water to thin the frosting to your desired consistency.

FM TIP: Cacao, rather than cocoa, is one of the leading anti-inflammatory foods. By including this, you're helping support the body to fight off any residual chronic inflammation you might have.

3-INGREDIENT CHOCOLATE MACADAMIA COOKIES

This recipe is from Peita, our Food Matters VP of Operations. It's her go-to recipe for the big and little kids in her house! It has the look and feel of a much-loved macadamia cookie, but instead of relying on butter, flour, and sugar, it lets the macadamias do all the hard work! They couldn't be easier, and they taste even better than the original.

SERVES: **12 TO 15**　　YIELD: **12 TO 15 COOKIES**　　PREP TIME: **10 MINUTES**　　COOK TIME: **12 MINUTES**

1 cup Medjool dates, pitted

1 cup macadamia nuts

1 tablespoon cacao powder

1. Preheat the oven to 350°F (180°C) and line a cookie tray with parchment paper.

2. Blend all the ingredients together to form the dough.

3. Scoop a tablespoon of the mixture, roll it into a ball in the palm of your hand, and place it on the lined cookie tray. Repeat, spacing the cookies 2 inches apart. Note: If you are having trouble rolling the cookie mixture, it helps to chill the mixture in the fridge for 10 minutes before rolling.

4. Bake for 10 to 12 minutes or until the cookies begin to brown, then remove from the oven.

FM TIP: Macadamia nuts are known to help lower bad cholesterol.[10] While most kids don't need to worry about this just yet, it makes these cookies a nourishing treat for adults too.

CHOCOLATE CHIP
OAT COOKIES

Chocolate chip cookies are always a crowd favorite among the kiddie critics. These healthified versions are hearty and nutritious, with the inclusion of oats, almond meal, and a sprinkle of sea salt flakes to enhance the flavor of each bite.

SERVES: **12 TO 15** | YIELD: **12 TO 15 COOKIES** | PREP TIME: **10 MINUTES** | COOK TIME: **10 MINUTES**

1 cup nut butter

⅔ cup coconut sugar

1 teaspoon vanilla extract

2 organic free-range eggs

1 cup gluten-free rolled oats

½ cup almond meal

½ teaspoon baking soda

⅔ cup vegan chocolate chips

Sea salt flakes for sprinkling (optional)

1. Preheat the oven to 350°F (180°C) and line a cookie tray with parchment paper.

2. Mix the nut butter, coconut sugar, vanilla extract, and eggs in a large bowl until smooth.

3. Add the rolled oats, almond meal, and baking soda, mix, then gently fold in the chocolate chips. The mixture should be a sticky consistency.

4. Roll about 2 tablespoons of the cookie mixture into a 2-inch ball and repeat, placing the balls on the lined baking tray about 2 inches apart.

5. Lightly flatten the cookies with your fingers or a fork.

6. Bake for 10 minutes or until the edges of the cookies just begin to brown. The cookies should be slightly undercooked, as they will continue to cook and harden once removed from the oven.

7. Optional: Sprinkle each cookie with sea salt flakes. Allow the cookies to cool completely before serving.

HEALTHY SNACKS

FM TIP: Cassava flour is a staple in the Food Matters kitchen! This root-derived flour is incredibly starchy, making it the perfect replacement for gluten's sticky texture.

ROSEMARY & SEA SALT CASSAVA CRACKERS

Making your own crackers at home is easier than you think. All you need is one bowl, five ingredients, and 30 minutes of your time. You'll be impressed with the crunchy product you end up with, which is perfect for dipping.

SERVES: 4	YIELD: 15 TO 18 CRACKERS	PREP TIME: 20 MINUTES	COOK TIME: 25 MINUTES

½ cup cassava flour

½ teaspoon unrefined sea salt, plus more for sprinkling

½ teaspoon dried rosemary

3 tablespoons extra virgin olive oil, plus more for rolling out dough

3 tablespoons warm water

1. Preheat the oven to 350°F (180°C) and line a baking tray with parchment paper.

2. In a bowl, mix the cassava flour, salt, and rosemary.

3. Make a well in the center of the dry mix and add the oil. Gradually add in 2 tablespoons water, adding more as necessary. You want the mixture to be combined well but sticky enough to create a dough-like consistency.

4. Place the dough in the refrigerator or freezer for 15 to 30 minutes. This will allow the dough to firm up and make it easier to handle.

5. Place a piece of parchment paper on your work surface and coat your hands in a small amount of olive oil to prevent the dough from sticking.

6. Scoop out the dough and flatten it on the parchment paper. Using a rolling pin or glass bottle, roll the dough as thinly as possible. Don't worry if it cracks a bit.

7. Place the rolled-out dough on the lined baking tray. Brush the dough with a little extra virgin olive oil, then sprinkle with salt.

8. Bake for 20 to 25 minutes or until it becomes golden and crisp.

9. Allow it to cool, then break into cracker pieces. Store in an airtight container.

ENERGY BLISS BALLS (4 WAYS)

Bliss balls are the answer to almost any of life's worries. They're a nutrient-packed option for snacks on the go, a pick-me-up during the 3 P.M. slump, or even a sweet treat before bed. But the best thing about bliss balls is that you can recreate all your favorite sweet flavors. These four recipes show you just how diverse they can be, including some that are nut-free.

COCONUT SALTED CARAMEL BLISS BALLS

SERVES: **15 TO 18**   YIELD: **15 TO 18 BALLS**

PREPARATION TIME: **20 MINUTES**   COOK TIME: **NONE**

- 1 cup Medjool dates, pitted, halved, and firmly packed
- 1 cup almond meal
- ¼ cup nut butter
- ¼ cup shredded coconut, plus more for rolling
- ¼ teaspoon unrefined sea salt
- ½ teaspoon vanilla extract

NUT-FREE CHOCOLATE BLISS BALLS

SERVES: **15 TO 18**   YIELD: **15 TO 18 BALLS**

PREPARATION TIME: **20 MINUTES**   COOK TIME: **NONE**

- ½ cup pepitas
- ½ cup sunflower seeds
- 2 tablespoons chia seeds
- 1 cup shredded coconut, plus more for rolling
- ¼ cup raw cacao powder
- 1 teaspoon ground cinnamon
- ¼ cup pure maple syrup
- 1 teaspoon vanilla extract
- ¼ cup melted coconut oil

1. In a blender or food processor, blend or process all the ingredients, except the coconut indicated for rolling, until the mixture is a sticky crumble.

2. Scoop out around 1 tablespoon of the mixture and roll into a 2-inch ball, then roll it in the shredded coconut. Place the ball on the baking sheet, repeat until all the mixture is used, and refrigerate until firm.

3. Store in an airtight container in the refrigerator for up to a month.

LEMON COCONUT TURMERIC BLISS BALLS

SERVES: **15 TO 18**   YIELD: **15 TO 18 BALLS**
PREPARATION TIME: **20 MINUTES**   COOK TIME: **NONE**

12 Medjool dates, pitted

1 cup gluten-free rolled oats

¼ cup activated almonds or cashews

4 tablespoons chia seeds

Juice of 1 lemon

1 teaspoon lemon zest

1 teaspoon vanilla extract

2 teaspoons ground turmeric

Shredded coconut, for rolling

NUT-FREE CHOC MINT ENERGY BALLS

SERVES: **15 TO 18**   YIELD: **15 TO 18 BALLS**
PREPARATION TIME: **20 MINUTES**   COOK TIME: **NONE**

⅔ cup sunflower seeds

⅓ cup pepitas

1 cup Medjool dates, pitted

1 cup sultanas

⅓ cup raw cacao powder

1 tablespoon

coconut oil

2 tablespoon pure maple syrup

4 drops food grade peppermint oil or 1 teaspoon peppermint essence

Shredded coconut, for rolling

FM TIP: Cauliflower is so nutrient-rich, we think it should be dubbed the next superfood! It's a rich source of fiber, micronutrients, and even antioxidants and phytonutrients that may protect against cancer.[11]

STICKY CRISPY CAULIFLOWER BITES

These cauliflower bites are the Food Matters take on buffalo wings. With a few staple spices, they've got the same kick that you know and love, but the substitution of cauliflower and an almond meal crumb will make them your new favorite veggie dish.

SERVES: **4** YIELD: **20 BITES** PREP TIME: **10 MINUTES** COOK TIME: **30 MINUTES**

CRISPY CAULIFLOWER

1 cup almond meal

1 teaspoon sweet smoked paprika

1 teaspoon ground cumin

½ teaspoon garlic powder

1 teaspoon ground turmeric

Unrefined sea salt and black pepper, to taste

1 cup unsweetened plant-based milk of choice (coconut, almond, oat)

½ cup brown rice flour

1 small head cauliflower, cut into bite-sized florets

STICKY SAUCE

½ cup tamari

4 tablespoons sriracha

2 tablespoons honey

1 tablespoon sesame oil

1 tablespoon rice wine vinegar

Unrefined sea salt and black pepper, to taste

1. Preheat the oven to 350°F (180°C) and line a baking tray with parchment paper.

2. Combine the almond meal, paprika, cumin, garlic powder, turmeric, salt, and pepper in a medium bowl to make a crumbly mixture.

3. In another bowl, mix the plant-based milk and brown rice flour to make the batter. Mix well.

4. Add the cauliflower florets to the brown rice flour batter, a few at a time, then toss the cauliflower in the almond meal spice crumble, coating well.

5. Spread the cauliflower on the lined baking tray and bake for 20 minutes or until the cauliflower begins to crisp.

6. While the cauliflower bakes, make the sticky sauce. Mix the tamari, sriracha, honey, sesame oil, rice wine vinegar, salt, and pepper in a small pot over medium heat. Stir continuously until the sauce begins to thicken. Remove from the heat.

7. Once the cauliflower is done baking, drizzle the sticky sauce over all the pieces, reserving 3 to 4 tablespoons of sauce.

8. Return the sauce-covered cauliflower to the oven and bake for another 8 to 10 minutes or until the sauce is sticky and browning.

9. Allow to slightly cool. Drizzle with the reserved sauce before serving.

GLUTEN-FREE BANANA BREAD

Banana bread has always been a kitchen hero, but we struggled to find any standout recipes that weren't laden with gluten. The few gluten-free recipes we found crumbled at the touch—and not in the good way! This recipe emerged as our own personal hero, and it's going to be yours now too . . .

SERVES: **8 TO 10**	YIELD: **8 TO 10 SLICES**	PREP TIME: **10 MINUTES**	COOK TIME: **40 MINUTES**

1 ½ **cups cassava flour**

1 **teaspoon baking soda**

½ **teaspoon unrefined sea salt**

¼ **teaspoon ground cinnamon**

3 **medium extra ripe bananas, mashed**

⅓ **cup extra virgin olive oil**

⅓ **cup pure maple syrup**

3 **organic free-range eggs**

2 **teaspoons vanilla extract**

3 **tablespoons unsweetened plant-based milk of choice (coconut, almond, oat)**

1. Preheat the oven to 350°F (180°C) and line a standard loaf pan with parchment paper.

2. Mix the cassava flour, baking soda, salt, and cinnamon in a large bowl.

3. Make a well in the center of the dry ingredients, and add the bananas, oil, maple syrup, eggs, vanilla extract, and plant-based milk.

4. Whisk together until combined well.

5. Pour the batter into the lined loaf pan and bake for 35 to 40 minutes, or until an inserted skewer comes out clean.

6. Allow the banana bread to cool slightly before removing and serving.

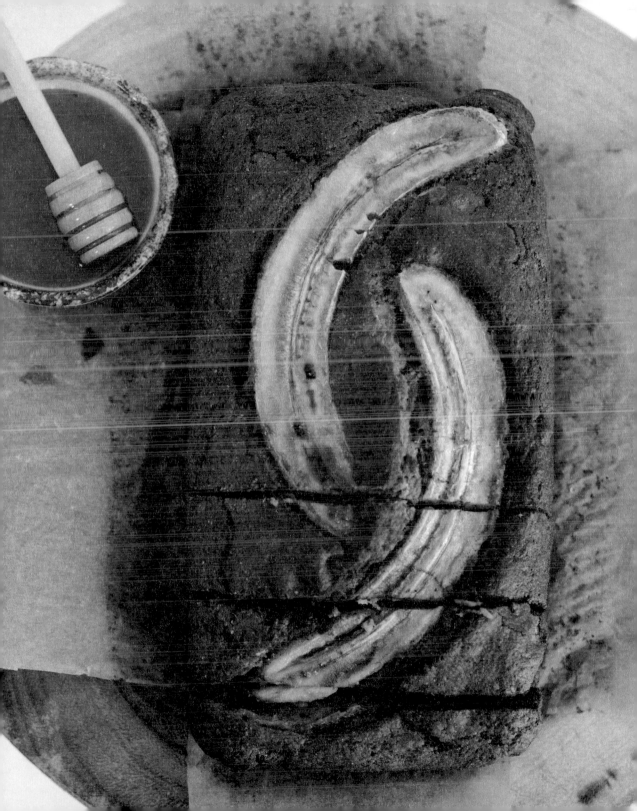

Our journey together doesn't just end here. Over the past 15 years, we've evolved Food Matters to be a space where we offer transformation for everyone, no matter where you're currently at. Whether you're just looking for more tips in the kitchen or are struggling with persistent gut issues, low energy, hormonal issues, or a long-term chronic condition, the food you eat (and avoid) can have an incredible effect on your body and well-being. We believe that with access to good-quality information, you can make better decisions to improve your health. From bliss ball beginner to green juice guru, we're here to support you with the tools and the knowledge you need to use the power of nutrition to heal yourself naturally.

> If you're looking for your next step on your health journey, then visit **www.foodmatters.com/bookbonus** for your exclusive *Food Matters Cookbook* gift.

On this page, you'll find a 7-Day Meal Plan and a free download from our Food Matters Nutrition Certification Program to help you make incorporating these healthy recipes into your life even easier.

We're thrilled you've made it this far! Remember, your journey is only just beginning and we can't wait to support you along the way.

In good health,

**JAMES COLQUHOUN &
LAURENTINE TEN BOSCH**

ONE-WEEK MEAL PLAN

WEEK 1	PREP DAY	MON	TUE
BREAKFAST	Prepare Chia Puddings (page 102) Chop and freeze bananas for smoothies	Coconut Blueberry Chia Pudding with Granola (page 102)	Food Matters Signature Green Smoothie (page 76)
LUNCH	Prepare Homemade Granola (page 216)	Skin Beauty Salad (page 238)	Super Green Pesto Pasta (page 191)
DINNER	Make Skin Beauty Salad Dressing (page 238)	Super Green Pesto Pasta (page 191)	Ginger & Cashew Veggie Stir-Fry (page 139)
SNACKS	Make Gluten-Free Banana Bread (page 334)	Gluten-Free Banana Bread (page 334)	Rosemary & Sea Salt Cassava Crackers w/ hummus (page 327)

If you're struggling to get started, we've created a seven-day meal plan to help you apply all the information in the book as easily as possible.

Here are some to suggestions to get you started with a full week of the recipes.

You'll find what you need to prep ahead of time in the prep-day column. A prep day isn't necessary, but it will make the rest of your week go more smoothly. This plan is designed for you to have leftovers from dinner for lunch the next day. Yum!

WED	THUR	FRI	SAT	SUN
Breakfast Taco with Homemade Gluten-Free Wrap (page 127)	Green Breakfast Bowl with Avocado (page 98)	Pineapple & Turmeric Anti-Inflammatory Smoothie (page 89)	Spinach & Harissa Shakshuka (page 122)	Food Matters 2-Ingredient Pancakes (page 105)
Ginger & Cashew Veggie Stir-Fry (page 119)	Everyday Chili Lime Fish Tacos (page 185) + Homemade Gluten-Free Wraps (page 220)	Rice Paper Rolls with Tamari Dipping Sauce (page 140)	Naked Burrito Bowl (page 143)	Bunless Beetroot Burger (page 146)
Everyday Chili Lime Fish Tacos (page 185) + Homemade Gluten-Free Wraps (page 220)	Rice Paper Rolls with Tamari Dipping Sauce (page 140)	Tray Bake Jackfruit Nachos with Charred Corn Salsa (page 192)	Bunless Beetroot Burger (page 146)	Clean Fish & Chips (page 175)
Gluten-Free Banana Bread (page 334)	Rosemary & Sea Salt Cassava Crackers w/ hummus (page 327)	Gluten-Free Banana Bread (page 334)	Nut Butter Fudge (page 303)	Nut Butter Fudge (page 303)

ENDNOTES

PART II

1. "Healthy Diets From Sustainable Food Systems – Food Planet Health," EAT-*Lancet* Commission Summary Report, 2019, https://eatforum.org/content/uploads/2019/07/EAT-Lancet_Commission_Summary_Report.pdf.

2. Nathan Fiala, "How Meat Contributes to Global Warming," *Scientific American*, February 2009, https://www.scientificamerican.com/article/the-greenhouse-hamburger/.

3. Amy Elizabeth, "The Meat Industry Wastes Water," PETA, last updated October 14, 2013, https://www.peta.org/blog/meat-industry-wastes-water/.

4. Tuso et al., "Nutritional Update for Physicians: Plant-Based Diets," *The Permanente Journal* 17, no. 2 (Spring 2013): 61–66.

5. Angelika Smidowicz and Julita Regula, "Effect of Nutritional Status and Dietary Patterns on Human Serum C-Reactive Protein and Interleukin-6 Concentrations," *Advances in Nutrition* 6, no. 6 (November 2015): 738–47.

6. Raeann Leal, "Is a Plant-Based Diet Good for Your Skin?," Life + Health Network, July 24, 2018, https://lifeandhealth.org/nutrition/is-a-plant-based-diet-good-for-your-skin/1711171.html.

7. Hope R. Ferdowsian and Neal D. Barnard, "Effects of Plant-Based Diets on Plasma Lipids," *The American Journal of Cardiology* 104, no. 7 (October 1, 2009): 947–56.

8. Ibid.

9. Satija et al., "Plant-Based Dietary Patterns and Incidence of Type 2 Diabetes in U.S. Men and Women: Results from Three Prospective Cohort Studies," *PLOS Medicine*, June 14, 2016, https://doi.org/10.137/journal.pmed.1002039.

10. Rock et al., "American Cancer Society Guideline for Diet and Physical Activity for Cancer Prevention," *A Cancer Journal for Clinicians* 70, no. 4 (July 2020): 245–71.

11. Katherine R. Groschwitz and Simon P. Hogan, "Intestinal Barrier Function: Molecular Regulation and Disease Pathogenesis," *Journal of Allergy and Clinical Immunology* 124, no. 1 (July 2009): 3–20.

12. Philip C. Calder, "Omega-3 Fatty Acids and Inflammatory Processes," *Nutrients* 2, no. 3 (March 2010): 355-74.

13. Institute of Medicine, "Relationships Among the Brain, the Digestive Systems, and Eating Behavior: Workshop Summary," The National Academies Press (February 2015).

14. Parra et al., "A Diet Rich in Long Chain Omega-3 Fatty Acids Modulates Satiety in Overweight and Obese Volunteers during Weight Loss," *Appetite* 51, no. 3 (November 2008): 676–80.

15. Tanja C. M. Adam, Johan Jocken, and Margriet S. Westertorp-Plantenga, "Decreased Glucagon-like Peptide 1 Release after Weight Loss in Overweight/Obese Subjects," *Obesity Research* 13, no. 4 (April 2005) 710–16.

16. Romilly E. Hodges and Deanna M. Minich, "Modulation of Metabolic Detoxification Pathways Using Foods and Food-Derived Components: A Scientific Review with Clinical Application," *Journal of Nutrition and Metabolism* 2015 (June 16, 2015), https://doi.org:10.1155/2015/760689.

17. Deborah A. Burton, Keith Stokes, and George M. Hall, "Physiological Effects of Exercise," *Continuing Education in Anaesthesia, Critical Care & Pain* 4, no. 6: 185–88.

18. Calder, "Omega-3 Fatty Acids and Inflammatory Processes," 355–74.

19. Rizvi et al., "The Role of Vitamin E in Human Health and Some Diseases," *Sultan Qaboos University Medical Journal* 14, no. 2 (May 2014): e157–65.

20. Sebastian J. Padayatty and Mark Levine, "Vitamin C Physiology: The Known and the Unknown and Goldilocks," *Oral Diseases* 22, no. 6 (September 2016): 463–93.

21. Martino F. Pengo, Christine H. Won, and Ghada Bourjeily, "Sleep in Women Across the Life Span," *Chest* 154, no. 1 (July 2018): 196–206.

22. Michalak et al., "Bioactive Compounds for Skin Health: A Review," *Nutrients* 13, no. 1 (January 12, 2021): 203.

23. Ibid.

24. Rizvi et al., "The Role of Vitamin E in Human Health," e157–65.

25. Michalak et al., "Bioactive Compounds for Skin Health," 203.

26. Ibid.

27. Rizvi et al., "The Role of Vitamin E in Human Health," e157–65.

28. Celestine Wong, Philip J. Harris, and Lynnette R. Ferguson, "Potential Benefits of Dietary Fiber Intervention in Inflammatory Bowel Disease," *International Journal of Molecular Sciences* 17, no. 6 (June 14, 2016): 919.

29. Bustamante et al., "Probiotics and Prebiotics Potential for the Care of Skin, Female Urogenital Tract, and Respiratory Tract," *Folia Microbiologica* 65, no. 2 (April 2020): 245–64.

30. Mark L. Dreher, "Whole Fruits and Fruit Fiber Emerging Health Effects," *Nutrients* 10, no. 12 (December 2018): 1833.

PART III

1. Giovanni De Pergola and Annunziata D'Alessandro, "Influence of Mediterranean Diet on Blood Pressure," *Nutrients* 10, no. 11 (November 2018): 1700.

2. Shyamala et al., "Studies on the Antioxidant Activities of Natural Vanilla Extract and its Constituent Compounds through in Vitro Models," *Journal of Agricultural and Food Chemistry* 55, no. 19 (October 2007): 7738–43.

3. Alasalvar et al., "Specialty Seeds: Nutrients, Bioactives, Bioavailability, and Health Benefits: A Comprehensive Review," *Comprehensive Reviews in Food Science and Food Safety* 20, no. 3 (May 2021): 2382–427.

4. Ibid.

5. Halima et al., "Antidiabetic and Antioxidant Effects of Apple Cider Vinegar on Normal and Streptozotocin-Induced Diabetic Rats," *International Journal for Vitamin and Nutrition*

Research 88, no. 5–6 (December 2018): 223–33.

6. Ng et al., "Curry Consumption and Cognitive Function in the Elderly," *American Journal of Epidemiology* 164 no. 9 (November 1, 2006): 898–906.

7. DiSilvestro et al., "Diverse Effects of a Low Dose Supplement of Lipidated Curcumin in Healthy Middle Aged People," *Nutrition Journal* 11, no. 79 (September 26, 2012), https://doi.org/10.1186/1475-2891-11-79.

8. Zare et al., "Effect of Cumin Powder on Body Composition and Lipid Profile in Overweight and Obese Women," *Complementary Therapies in Clinical Practice* 20, no. 4 (November 2014): 297–301.

9. Laura L. Laslett and Graeme Jones, "Capsaicin for Osteoarthritis Pain," *Progress in Drug Research* 68 (2014): 277–91.

10. Kim et al., "Binding, Antioxidant and Anti-proliferative Properties of Bioactive Compounds of Sweet Paprika," *Plant Foods for Human Nutrition* 71, no. 2 (June 2016): 129–36.

11. T. Alan Jiang, "Health Benefits of Culinary Herbs and Spices," *Journal of AOAC International* 102, no. 2 (March 2019): 395–411.

12. Ibid.

13. Zheng et al., "Spices for Prevention and Treatment of Cancers," *Nutrients* 8, no. 8 (August 2016): 495.

14. Jiang, "Health Benefits of Culinary Herbs and Spices," 395–411.

15. Ibid.

16. Ibid.

17. Ehab A. Abourashed and Abir T. El-Alfy, "Chemical Diversity and Pharmacological Significance of the Secondary Metabolites of Nutmeg," *Phytochemistry Reviews* 15, no. 6 (December 2016): 1035–56.

18. Ibid.

19. Deen et al., "Chemical Composition and Health Benefits of Coconut Oil: An Overview," *Journal of the Science of Food and Agriculture* 101, no. 6 (April 2021): 2182–93.

20. Yubero-Serrano et al., "Extra Virgin Olive Oil: More than a Healthy Fat," *European Journal of Clinical Nutrition* 72, supplement 1 (July 2019): 8–17.

21. Knowles et al., "Adding Nutritional Value to Meat and Milk from Pasture-Fed Livestock," *New Zealand Veterinary Journal* 52, no. 6 (December 2004): 342–51.

22. Ibid.

23. Srihari Mahadov and Peter H. R. Green, "Celiac Disease," *Gastroenterology & Hepatology* 7, no. 8 (August 2011): 554–56.

24. Ibid.

25. Ibid.

26. Baião et al., "Polyphenols from Root, Tubercles and Grains Cropped in Brazil: Chemical and Nutritional Characterization and Their Effects on Human Health and Diseases," *Nutrients* 9, no. 9 (September 2017): 1044.

27. Lee-Kwan et al., "Disparities in State-Specific Adult Fruit and Vegetable Consumption—United States, 2015," *Morbidity and Mortality Weekly Report* 66, no. 45 (November 2017): 1241–47.

PART IV

1. Que et al., "Advances in Research on the Carrot, an Important Root Vegetable in the Apiaceae Family," *Horticulture Research* 6 (June 1, 2019): 69.

2. Domínguez et al., "Effects of Beetroot Juice Supplementation on Intermittent High-Intensity Exercise Efforts," *Journal of the International Society of Sports Nutrition* 15 (January 5, 2018): 2..

3. Allam et al., "Protective Effect of Parsley Juice (*Petroselinum crispum*, Apiaceae) against Cadmium Deleterious Changes in

the Developed Albino Mice Newborns (*Mus musculus*) Brain," *Oxidative Medicine and Cell Longevity* 2016 (December 2015).

4. Duthie et al., "Effect of Increasing Fruit and Vegetable Intake by Dietary Intervention on Nutritional Biomarkers and Attitudes to Dietary Change: A Randomised Trial," *European Journal of Nutrition* 57, no. 5 (August 2018): 1855–72.

5. Grzybek et al., "Evaluation of Anthelmintic Activity and Composition of Pumpkin (*Cucurbita pepo L.*) Seed Extracts—In Vitro and In Vivo Studies," *International Journal of Molecular Sciences* 17, no. 9 (September 1, 2016): 1456.

6. Colpo et al., "Brazilian Nut Consumption by Healthy Volunteers Improves Inflammatory Parameters," *Nutrition* 30, no. 4 (April 2014): 459–65.

7. Rupasinghe et al., "Industrial Hemp (*Cannabis sativa* subsp. *sativa*) as an Emerging Source for Value-Added Functional Food Ingredients and Nutraceuticals," *Molecules* 25, no. 18 (September 7, 2020): 4078.

8. Salehi et al., "Antioxidant, Antimicrobial, and Anticancer Effects of *Anacardium* Plants: An Ethnopharmacological Perspective," *Frontiers in Endocrinology* 11 (June 2020): 295.

9. Abbaoui, et al., "Cruciferous Vegetables, Isothiocyanates, and Bladder Cancer Prevention," *Molecular Nutrition & Food Research* 62, no. 18 (September 2018): e1800079.

10. Schwingshackl et al., "Food Groups and Intermediate Disease Markers: A Systematic Review and Network Meta-analysis of Randomized Trials," *The American Journal of Clinical Nutrition* 108, no. 3 (September 2018): 576–86.

11. Abbaoui et al., "Cruciferous Vegetables, Isothiocyanates, and Bladder Cancer Prevention," e1800079.

INDEX

NOTE: Page references in *italics* refer to photos of recipes.

ABOUT THE AUTHORS

JAMES COLQUHOUN & LAURENTINE TEN BOSCH are the filmmaking duo behind *Food Matters*, *Hungry for Change*, and *Transcendence* seasons 1 and 2 and the founders of Food Matters and FMTV. Together they founded the Food Matters community to help give people the tools (films, books, articles, and guided programs) to take charge of their own health. You can visit them online at www.foodmatters.com.

HAY HOUSE TITLES
OF RELATED INTEREST

We hope you enjoyed this Hay House book. If you'd like to receive our online catalog featuring additional information on Hay House books and products, or if you'd like to find out more about the Hay Foundation, please contact:

Hay House, Inc., P.O. Box 5100, Carlsbad, CA 92018-5100
(760) 431-7695 or (800) 654-5126
(760) 431-6948 (fax) or (800) 650-5115 (fax)
www.hayhouse.com® • www.hayfoundation.org

———

Published in Australia by: Hay House Australia Pty. Ltd.,
18/36 Ralph St., Alexandria NSW 2015
Phone: 612-9669-4299 • *Fax:* 612-9669-4144
www.hayhouse.com.au

Published in the United Kingdom by: Hay House UK, Ltd.,
The Sixth Floor, Watson House, 54 Baker Street, London W1U 7BU
Phone: +44 (0)20 3927 7290 • *Fax:* +44 (0)20 3927 7291
www.hayhouse.co.uk

Published in India by: Hay House Publishers India,
Muskaan Complex, Plot No. 3, B-2, Vasant Kunj, New Delhi 110 070
Phone: 91-11-4176-1620 • *Fax:* 91-11-4176-1630
www.hayhouse.co.in

———

<u>Access New Knowledge.</u>
<u>Anytime. Anywhere.</u>

Learn and evolve at your own pace
with the world's leading experts.

www.hayhouseU.com

Listen. Learn. Transform.

Embrace vibrant, lasting health with unlimited Hay House audios!

Unlock endless wisdom, fresh perspectives, and life-changing tools from world-renowned authors and teachers—helping you live your happiest, healthiest life. With the *Hay House Unlimited Audio* app, you can learn and grow in a way that fits your lifestyle . . . and your daily schedule.

With your membership, you can:

- Develop a healthier mind, body, and spirit through natural remedies, healthy foods, and powerful healing practices.

- Explore thousands of audiobooks, meditations, immersive learning programs, podcasts, and more.

- Access exclusive audios you won't find anywhere else.

- Experience completely unlimited listening. No credits. No limits. No kidding.

Try for FREE!

AUDIO
UNLIMITED

Visit **hayhouse.com/try-free** to start your free trial and get one step closer to living your best life.